SOONER OR LATER

SOONER OR LATER

TALES OF
A PIONEER FAMILY

VIRGINIA STUMBOUGH

Virginia Stumbough
for Audrey Theobald

Clear Light Publishers
Santa Fe, New Mexico

Clear Light Publishers, 823 Don Diego Santa Fe, New Mexico 87501

Library of Congress Cataloging-in-Publication Data

Stumbough, Virginia Carter. 1910-
    Sooner or later : tales of a western pioneer family / Virginia Stumbough.
    p. cm.
    ISBN 0-940666-25-1 : $12.95
    1. Stumbough family. 2. Hawkins family. 3. Keegan family. 4. Oklahoma—Biography. 6. Frontier and pioneer life—Oklahoma. I. Title
CT274. S79S78 1993   92-41761
929' .2'0973—dc20   CIP

First Printing
10 9 8 7 6 5 4 3 2 1

Printed in U.S.A.
Baker Johnson, Dexter, Michigan

Contents

Preface

APROFESSOR FROM THE South recently said that we are at least fiftieth cousins to every living person on all continents of the earth. This tells us that there isn't a family line anywhere which doesn't include the famous and infamous, saint and sinner, and a lot of just plain, fascinating oddballs.

Back in the days when rural roads weren't paved, a female cousin who was a dwarf held the post of tollgate keeper for a corduroy road — that is, a road built of logs to keep cars and trucks from sinking into the mud during the rainy season. A lighthouse keeper cousin died while his wife was visiting, leaving her there alone with his body for a week before anyone was due to come and fetch her.

Oshea Stowell from Brookline, Massachusetts, well-educated and of good family, moved to Monroe, Michigan, and prospered there as an outstanding and exemplary member of the church. In 1823 he wooed and won Mary Mulholland, one of my ancestors. He was thought to be a real catch for Mary, who at twenty-six years of age, was considered an old-maid schoolmarm. They had two babies and settled down to married life on a farm.

One day Oshea went to town with a considerable amount of money, both his own and the neighbors', to buy necessary supplies. He was never heard from again, and Mary mourned for him all her life, feeling certain that he had been robbed and killed by Indians en route, though his body was never found. Many years later her children were approached by a lawyer, who sought their signatures on a release that would enable Oshea's wife and heirs in Canada to inherit his estate. Mary's children never told her what had actually happened to him.

Another dastardly heartbreaker was William Hugh Lothian of the Lothian Estates in Scotland. Having deserted a wife and son in Scotland, he kept his past well-hidden, eventually prospering in a rural community in Indiana. He married Angeline Clifford of my Davidson line and seemed to settle down. Angeline was outraged, however, when he ran off with the maid, and married her under the name of William King. Angeline divorced him and remarried. Their two children, learning the true story later on, took both names, Lothian and King.

Cousin Joseph Hodges Choate was named United States Ambassador to Britain, and there is a statue of cousin Rufus Choate standing in Boston, as tribute to the great statesman that he was. In our Carter family tree the tendrils of kinship connect us back to near relatives of Martha, wife of President George Washington.

A relative from Washington state was born to an aging Civil War veteran and a somewhat unstable young mother who tried to rob a bank on the grounds that it was locked when she wanted to withdraw her money. She was hospitalized, leaving her young daughter to make her own decisions. She worked in a factory at the age of fifteen, and then married young. She saved her money, paid fifty dollars for a house, and painted it herself, both inside and out. Then she persuaded her husband, a charmer who preferred fishing and hunting to working, to do some carpentry. Through such enterprise they were able to sell their home at a profit and immediately invest in a larger one. This hard-working woman repeated the process the rest of her life. She died a few years ago, leaving a considerable estate to her children.

There isn't a reader of this book who isn't related in some degree to the writer and all of the people mentioned above, as well as to countless other interesting persons in his or her own line.

Welcome cousin; see you at the annual family picnic.

HERITAGE

I am, but not.
I shiver in spray, quiver toward dimness,
   watch continent passed from sight,
   beyond seething waves under bowsprit perch.
I trek on foot through black leaf tunnels,
   Quaker hand on powder-horn,
   yearning away from peace toward plenty.
My nostrils sting at stench of bog and swamp.
Eyes half-blinded, staring, strain past
   prairies, plains and peaks;
   dust, mirage, dry seas of hip-high grass.
My roughened hands, gently trained in dainty
   needlework,
   smash rattlers, snatch young from danger,
   hold stubbornly to one last shred of beauty.
I weave, I reap, I patch and hew.
I blast a living thing to death;
   I bring a living thing to breath.
I am one, but all:
   Carter, Hawkins, Keegan, Makins;
   Mulholland, Sullivan, Chenoweth, Choate;
   Lawson, Manning, Eagy, Davidson;
   Cornwall, Wiley, Calvert, Cook
American potage, potently spiced.
Ghostly shadow, I move at their will,
   At their impulse act.
I am, they are — will always be.
I am, but not.

             — Virginia Stumbough

Introduction

THE STORIES OF OUR forefathers are not anchors tying us to certain lifestyles, smothering us with warnings: "That's not the way we do things in our family." Rather, they are springboards, inspiration to venture out into the new and untried, the often scary pathways of our own choosing. The more we learn of their examples, the more eager we are to surge ahead. We choose our own signposts, but our forefathers have broken the way. Mother used to remind us that we could learn something from everyone, including the so-called bad examples. Ancient wisdom teaches that every stumbling block is a steppingstone if we make it so. I think my ancestors did this. You'll see it again and again as you share our stories.

This book is American history as it was lived: family stories, which are the basic material of all histories. The stories have been collected not only over my own long lifetime, but have been written down and passed on to me by my parents, grandparents, and even great-grandparents. We are a long-lived clan, given to letter writing and keeping scrapbooks. All these personal recollections and documents, the letters and memoirs of Western pioneer folk, have tended to gravitate to me because I am a journalist, and because I cherish them so.

My ancestors' recollections are occasionally funny. Some people have been famous, some infamous. The bottom line is that we are always just plain folks, not one whit more important or interesting than any other family. However, family stories shape our lives for good or ill, wherever they have been told. I am a product of my fam-

1

ily, willy-nilly: I feel that they are some small part of me in every breath I take. As one of my early college professors said, "Man is a verbal animal; writing is his record, by which he hands experience from generation to generation, increasing his choice of action in any given situation a thousand-fold."*

Indeed, there is a human quality which separates us from the eternal present of the animal kingdom. We can look into the past, learn of the trials and triumphs of our forefathers, see the interweaving of our lives with theirs, and thus inform our vision of the present and future. It is in that sense that there are riches to be mined from gathering family remembrances.

Tradition, roots, and personal history — all instilled and preserved in the cultures of Europe, Asia, and the indigenous American Indians — these are riches that are often neglected today, when we have more immediate and pressing concerns. Remembering our heritage gives us a sense of personal worth and dignity. In appreciating the stories of our ancestors, we are inspired to look outward, and practice a like respect for all that lives.

---

* Baker Brownell, *The New Universe* (New York: D. Van Nostrand Co., Inc., 1926).

Famous and Infamous:
Sir John Hawkins

THOUGH NOT TO BE bragged about particularly, our most renowned early day family member was probably Lord Admiral Sir John Hawkins (1532–1595), founder of the slave trade in England during the reign of Queen Elizabeth I.

The Hawkins family were ship owners in Plymouth and maintained a large part of the British fleet. Serving under his distant and younger cousin Sir Francis Drake, John Hawkins headed one of the English squadrons in the battle which defeated the Spanish Armada. Notwithstanding the fact that it was the luck of a storm that finally destroyed the Spanish fleet at sea and thus saved the English ships, the Queen honored Admiral Hawkins by knighting him and naming him Comptroller of the English Navy. Armed with the Queen's help and blessing in founding the slave trade, he was hugely successful in breaking up Spain's stronghold on the exploitation of the New World. Feared and hated over there, he was much lauded at home.

In a letter to Queen Elizabeth, Sir John writes of "sundry instruments of music for eight musicians and nine trumpeters." He also mentions a new form of nourishment introduced by a man named Hugh Platt: a type of food fashioned in the "form of hollow pipes." These curiously shaped "lasting victuals" were called "macaroni."

In 1625, Samuel Purchas, a chronicler of the times, wrote that the dispositions of Sir John Hawkins and Sir Francis Drake were so contrary to one another, that what

3

one man wanted the other would usually oppose. The former had "a plodding caution" which must have sorely clashed with "the careless and eventually wild opportunism" of the latter's youth.* Of Hawkins, Purchas wrote that he was slow, jealous, rude, contentious, ambitious, and found it hard to make up his mind. Though Purchas found Drake to be the better man, he also allowed that Hawkins was merciful and forgiving, honest in speech, patient with crew members, discreet in danger, and hardworking.

Slaver, smuggler, privateer, and adventurer, Hawkins was not always successful in his ventures. In 1568 his slave ships were near the coast of Mexico. While attempting to trade slaves for gold, he shot cannons at the Spanish in Veracruz. Their response was to set his ships afire, and Hawkins was obliged to limp back to England with only one small damaged vessel, with neither slaves nor loot aboard.

Years later the admiral died aboard ship off the coast of Puerto Rico. Some said it was a fever that killed him, but according to a more romantic version, others said he died of grief at the unsuccessful conclusion of a voyage he'd undertaken in a search for treasures. In his own words: "If I had any enemy, I would wish him no more harm than the course of my troublesome and painful life, but hereunto, and to God's good Providence, we are born."

Sir John Hawkins' crest was a Moor in chains. His title, castle, and fortune, all granted to him by the Queen, were perhaps ill-gotten "honors" in the light of today's

---

* Kenneth R. Andrews, *The Last Voyage of Drake and Hawkins*, Haklyt Society, vol. 142 (Cambridge: Cambridge University Press, 1972).

rather more enlightened attitudes. But according to attitudes commonly held at the time John Hawkins lived, he was considered a benefactor to mankind for having converted "pagans" to Christianity, thus saving them from hellfire. This trampling on the dignity of human beings of a different culture renders our famous ancestor an infamous one by today's standards. Nonetheless, he remains an original, with a powerful presence.

Sir John Hawkins, smuggler, adventurer, and English patriot. From the collection of the National Maritime Museum.

The Galleon of Don Pedro taken Prisoner by Sr Francis Drake, and sent to Dartmouth.

Nearly a hundred years after the event, the Armada playing-card achieves a more realistic version of the loss of the Rosario than the near-contemporary image-makers, but with the sacrifice of drama.

Witchcraft

DURING THE SEVENTEENTH century, terror of "witch-craft" and the senseless and rabid persecution of women accused of practicing it gripped New England. Cotton Mather, the respected clergyman who wrote more than four hundred works for the spiritual benefit of his flock, was a tragically misguided moralist. He bore a major responsibility for provoking the popular frenzy over "the evils of witchcraft." In 1692, after hideous torture, twenty so-called witches were hanged and one hundred and fifty other women were imprisoned in Salem, Massachusetts.

Yet in the midst of the madness, when even to associate with anyone accused of witchcraft was to put one's own life in danger, one of our forefathers, a Wentworth Day of Boston, is recorded as honorably saving "a woman charged with the horrid office." Day, a surgeon practicing medicine in Cambridge, Massachusetts in 1640, stood up in public and used all his prestige and persuasion to prove that the accused woman was not a witch. She was not convicted.

This true and inspirational three-hundred-year-old story has been so cherished within the family that it has come down to us today through seven generations of the Day, Choate, Mulholland, and Keegan families. I'm proud to be able to tell it once more.

1816: The Year of No Summer

IN THE YEAR 1816, Mount Tambora in Indonesia erupted and wind currents spread a thick cloud of volcanic ash which affected vast areas all over the earth. The solid banks of dust blocked both the sunlight and the westerly flow of winds, allowing polar air to penetrate far to the south. The effects were devastating. There were almost no crops, and in England, where my ancestors were about to flee from the political and social oppression of the times, snow fell every month of the year. Plants perished, animals and people died of starvation.

In England, melons rotted in their frames and never ripened. Hay failed. People ate nettles, wild turnips and turkeys, hedgehogs, anything they could find. Sheep already sheared had to have their fleece tied around them again to prevent their freezing to death. Leaves withered and trees did not leaf again that year. Some winter grain made a crop, but much wheat was harvested in the milk. It had to be baked in an oven, and then mashed into dough or boiled like rice. People who could afford it bought imported grain, flour, and fish — all sold at fantastic prices.

Typhoid fever was another plague of the times. The drains made of lead pipe were seamed at the sides and connected to cisterns, which were infrequently cleaned. Swine rutted in rotting vegetables in the street, and the putrid air and lack of sanitation led to cholera epidemics.

During 1812, when Britain and America were at war, the whole economy of England changed. The passing of the restrictive corn law in 1815 contributed to unemployment, intolerable taxation, and labor unrest. Revolution became a real danger. Indeed, no city property was safe, thieves were seldom caught, and householders were often slain by robbers. Landed gentry, who protected their laborers, were wiped out by taxation and were replaced by profiteers. A cow worth fifteen cents in 1813 dropped in value to three cents by 1822. As a further devastation to the economy, the 1816 tariff law passed in the United States hampered English export trade with import duties.

All but one of the descendants of my great-great grandfather William Hawkins ended up in America essentially because a volcano spread a layer of dust over the earth, England was suffering from a generation of industrial, economic, and political strife, and William was a younger brother who, according to English custom, was unable to inherit any of the family's wealth. Too, William sought a healthier climate for his wife who was very ill.

Fleeing the illness and hard times of England, the Hawkins, among our first ancestors to take up a life in North America, emigrated to Montreal in 1816, "The Year of No Summer." The mother of the family survived the rigors of the ocean journey by only a few weeks.

The threat of revolution in England continued for a number of years, as attested to in a letter that William Hawkins received from his brother-in-law in 1830, fourteen years after the Hawkins family had emigrated to America. The brother-in-law, Jonathon Hodgson, ends his grim letter describing an England racked with poverty, with the following comment: "So from this, I will leave you to judge the state of old England, giving you a hint that a revolution is talked of in many parts."

George Hawkins

GEORGE HAWKINS, SON OF William, was ten years old when he sailed with his father, mother, and two sisters from Hull, England, to North America in the late summer or fall of 1816. His father had originally made arrangements to cross the Atlantic in a fair-sized sailing ship, probably a packet ship of about seventy tons. He changed his mind and canceled the booking, later learning that she had gone down with the loss of all on board.

The ship the family crossed in was "an oldish one, on her last trip for passengers," said George when he dictated his life story to his grandson Roy Hoffman, nearly eighty years later. "I heard them say we had head winds all the way."

Boarding the ship, the Hawkins family probably had to pay the custom officers the usual bribe of a shilling or so, to prevent the bother of opening and unpacking their trunks and other baggage for inspection. The family had a cabin together, perhaps in steerage, since it only cost about a pound and a half to obtain berths, fire, and water. The roomier first class was thirty pounds. Considering the times, that was a very large amount.

In both cases, back then one had to furnish one's own provisions and bedding. Common ship's fare was biscuits, pickled tripe, and salt beef, with passengers sharing with each other whatever they had brought. There may have been a cow on board, which would have provided milk, and perhaps the ship carried salt herring in a tub.

The voyage probably took thirty to forty days or more, even going the short way via Quebec and Montreal instead of New York. The crossing was dreadful, stormy and rough. They took rhubarb or epsom salts for seasickness, but still spent much time in their bunks, trying to keep from losing their food and being tossed out of their beds.

Said George, in telling his story to Roy, "I wanted to be a sailor until we had a great storm. The sailors were drenched with water. Their feet seemed to be almost in the ocean while they were taking in sails. The storm tore the main sail, split the main mast, and tore away the jib, which was lost. The sailors made another one.

"We were shut down in the hold. We could hear the captain's trumpet, and thought it was Gabriel's, we were so scared. I thought the big fish would break through the deck and swallow me, and hoped that they wouldn't. We all three stayed in our bunk, Pa was up all night keeping things from breaking.

"When reefing and taking in the sails, one of the sailors fell in the ocean. A jolly boat was sent immediately to his rescue. He swam to the buoy and held on until it reached him; he was a noble swimmer. We were scudding at fourteen knots an hour, I heard them say."

Fourteen knots is about sixteen land miles an hour, but George probably had never gone faster than a good horse could carry him on the rough stone lanes of the English countryside. Now he literally flew across the waves, blown bouncing and rocking from the top of one tremendous upheaval of water to another. Their lives depended utterly on the captain's and crew's skill, for without that and a sound hull they could only drown.

But not all the journey was rough.

"I went and sat on the bowsprit," George continued, "so the foam would touch my feet, but a sailor said he was afraid I would fall off and that I must not go there no

George Hawkin: His Story

(1806 - 1896)

11

more. That scared me and I left and went to climbing the rope ladders, and the sailor came again and said he was afraid I would fall. Well, I went to my marbles then, of course."

George's father, a younger son who could not inherit, had been taught the stone mason's trade, and among other things he made marbles. His son was probably an expert player, though one wonders how he managed the game on a heaving ship.

George continued his story, describing their final approach to the New World: "We had to tack until we got to the channel, then we had to wait two or three days for the pilot who was taking in another vessel to the port. You always must have a pilot; he knows where the obstructions lie and how to steer to keep clear of them. Our pilot took hold of the wheel then, and ran her into port."

The pilot, in a spruce little boat, had rejoined them at Father Point at the mouth of the St. Lawrence River, bringing them eagerly sought newspapers. The Hawkins family then traveled by steamer, from Tadoussac to Montreal, and beheld for the first time the river banks lined with French-Canadian farmhouses. Since the only roadway was the river, each wooden house faced the water at the end of a long, narrow piece of farmland. The Hawkins family eagerly took in the whitewashed cottages, tin church spires glistening above the green treetops, and the tall flagpoles marking the residences of militia officers. It was a mighty and spacious contrast to what they had known back in England, where the snug, stone cottages nestled safely behind wide hedgerows.

It took twenty to thirty hours to cover the hundred and seventy miles up the St. Lawrence from Quebec to Mont-

Abigail Jane Davidson, George's wife, always called Jane because of other Abigails in the family, was a skilled weaver. I still use one of her blue and white coverlets, which she wove over 150 years ago.

real. The river was calm, majestic, and silent. Approach-Approaching Montreal, George described his first impressions:

"Near the harbor the Indians and Canadians were paddling in the water and jabbering bad words. I learned what one word was which they said so often, 'sacre' (cursed, or damned). They were a wonderful people to swear. I found that out afterwards when I went to school at Montreal. I have seen them pull off almost all of their clothes and fight until the blood would flow, which of course scared me very much. Well, I got to be a fighter too, and got whipped first thing, but I was bound to defend myself any way if I could, and never was afraid of anyone but SATAN."

Docking at Montreal, they were surrounded by merchant ships, rafts, ferry boats, and small craft. George and his father wrestled their iron-bound calfskin trunk with its big brass lock down the gangplank to the dock. They encountered blanket-clad Indians selling moccasins, belts, bark work, and fine leather tobacco pouches. There were old French-Canadians with long pigtails tied up with eel-skins and sailors from distant lands dressed in all kinds of outlandish costumes. A babble of tongues filled the air, and George swore to himself then that someday he would learn the language of the land. Eighty years later and hundreds of miles away in the Wabash Valley of Indiana, he still spoke French with great pride in his accomplishment.

Montreal, 1816–1821

IN 1816 MONTREAL WAS a somnolent old French town with a population of about 15,000 people — dirty, flower-decked, reeking of garlic, soft with the sound of church bells.

Enclosed by great stone walls, the city boasted the fine Gothic church of Notre Dame, not yet finished; a new Anglican Christ Church; several convents; a library and a newspaper; the old rambling structure of the Château de Ramezy; and the "haunted" unfinished mansion of Simon McTavich. Opposite the city stretched a flat plain, and on the horizon rose the bold outline of the Vermont and New York mountains.

Forty feet below the great walls of the city fortification were the pastures of the common and the river front. Below, too, spread the crumbling earthworks of the ancient French fort of St. John's. In 1852 the town was said to be "the dirtiest place in America, unequaled in public and private nuisances, and wanting in common conveniences, obnoxious to health and decency." The streets were filthy and irregular, narrow and ill-paved. A deep open ditch ran along the street behind the river front, a receptacle for every kind of noxious garbage. The old French market square by the river front on Craig Street was in a damp, unpleasant hollow.

Molson's private wharf handled steamers for Quebec and La Prairie and was a station for stages traveling to St. John and the States. A weekly stage also left St. John's Gate in Upper Town every Sunday morning for the six-day journey to Boston. There were no public wharves. Ships were tied up along the river bank where currents had scooped the water deep, and stages were built out from the shore's edge to the decks of the ships. Where the water was shallow horses could pull carts out into the river to the ships' bows.

Hauled up along the river bank were *bateaux*, big Durham boats, and flat-bottomed sailboats eighty to ninety feet long with center boards which enabled them to beat to windward. Many rafts crowded the harbor, filled with firewood: cordwood for town use brought down from the farms upriver, as well as square timber bound for Quebec and England. This was Canada's great harbor, its gateway to the ocean.

About two thousand five hundred houses lined the hundred streets, with water laid in to them through pipes leading from a mountain pond. In dry weather there was too little water and in wet weather there was too much, so that in summer the pipes dried and in winter they burst. Water was then pumped from wells or hauled in carts from the river. By law, every house had to have its own fire ladders and buckets.

Except for the glow of whale-oil lamps here and there, the streets were unlit at night. There was no night watchman or policeman, nor any city government except for justices of the peace and military authorities. Medical facilities were scant, so the thousands of immigrants stricken with disease as soon as they landed had slim chance of being treated. Others got drunk and stayed that way.

The bank of Montreal didn't open until the year after the family arrived, but with a flourishing street market and river trade, as well as many stores selling goods of all kinds, there was a lively commerce in the city.

Dry goods stores sold fur caps, bonnets, muffs, tippets, pelereens (capes), boas, and stocks. Shoemakers displayed Russian long boots; cabinet makers sold feather beds; tailors offered broadcloths, saccimeres, and vestings. There were silk mercers, drapers, and haberdashers, dry grocers, tallow chandlers, black and white smiths, wig and curl makers, and staymakers. There were dealers in potash and pearl-ash, as well as in muskrat and bear skins. Apothecary shops sold drugs, soaps, perfumes, unguents, dye-stuffs, painters' colors, Indian moccasins, costumes and curios, pickles, spices, and sauces.

We can imagine the arrival of the Hawkins family in Montreal one afternoon in the autumn of 1816, and the excitement with which they may have beheld this foreign marketplace: farmers standing by their carts, vending grain and vegetables, baskets, eggs, cheese, butter, maple sugar, dressed fowls, bags of flour, fresh fish, and live geese; women sitting with their baskets spread about them, bartering homespun fabrics, linen, socks, crocheted shawls, rag carpets, woolen mittens, red toques, and flannels; Indians dressed in knee-length leather jackets and leggings, the women carrying their babies on their backs, trading Indian baskets, moccasins, toboggans and snowshoes.

This was the city that George Hawkins and his family lived in when they first came to America.

One hundred and sixty pupils, aged from eight to ten years old, studied at the Petit Seminarie in the Ricollet suburb outside the Ricollet Gate, one and a half miles from the Hawkins' home. It was the only school in town, and all classes were taught in French by the Sulpician Brothers. George was studying there when his mother passed away on December 11, 1816:

"When we arrived [in Montreal], Ma was not well at all [even] then, and she died in about six weeks after we arrived in the city. We had crossed the ocean for health as much as anything, I heard Father say. I felt quite bad next morning when Pa said at night after we got home from Seminary, 'Your Ma is dead, now you won't have to go and tell the doctor to come any more on her account.' I did not like to go after the doctor."

There was no English hospital in Montreal at that time; the House of Recovery, at the corner of St. Joseph and Gabriel Streets, had a mere four rooms and a single doctor in charge. Most families looked after their own sick members, occasionally calling on the doctors who lived in the neighborhoods of three particular streets.

George continued:

"We lived five years in the city, then my father was remarried in the English Church. Neither myself or sisters knew anything of it until he brought his wife home one evening, along with the bridesmaid and another, and introduced us to our new mama. Well, we all three of us kissed her, and had a good time that evening. They put me upstairs where I caught the croup that night, and came near dying, but my new Ma gave me something to ease me, and it helped me to breathe better."

William and Abigail Pease (1798–1882) were wed on March 11, 1817. According to family tradition, Abigail, who had some Indian blood, was a descendant of Pocahontas. Certainly her children and grandchildren all retained the look of Indians, with high cheek bones and dark skin and hair. William and Abigail had eleven children in the course of their

18

marriage, and eventually moved the family to South Hero, Vermont, Abigail's birthplace.

In George's account of the rest of the years that the Hawkins family remained in Montreal, it is a little difficult to arrange every episode in chronological order, with proper dates. One incident George described occurred on a bitter cold night:

"When I got out one night before going to bed, I heard a groan. I went in and told Father, who was at home then, and he went out and brought in a man almost frozen to death. We got the wash tub out to thaw out his hands and legs and feet. How I did pity him! He suffered so much night and day. He was a deserter and had walked from the barracks of Montreal. The snow was heavy and deep, and he had laid down to rest. This was his third attempt, and it was death if he was caught. The sergeant came after him in a carriage, cured him up, and hustled him off. As I afterwards heard, he had him shot."

George also described the evening when his father's house burned down:

"Then when Pa got burnt out I had to go to work. When I first saw Pa's house on fire, the cloth was spread all ready for supper. I had just gone to the wood house for wood, and saw the blaze coming out of the roof. I got no supper that night.

"I had a dog-harness in a barrel, and carried it across the road out of danger. The fire bells began to ring, and the men came and began to throw things every way, while I stood at the other side of the road. It was very funny for me until we had to go, after it was all over, a mile through town to a cousin of my father's for the night.

"The fire was the ruination of him [William], and when I found out of course I was grieved. I heard him tell his wife that he had been offered a big price for the property and if it was worth that to someone else, it was worth that to him. The building was brick, two stories, tin roof. Had a small insurance, which we got."

Houses in Montreal at that time were built of wood, stone, rubble-stone or brick, usually with tin roofs and door shutters cased in sheet iron. They were hot in summer, with a furnace-like atmosphere because of the tin roof. The French-Canadian farmhouses along the rivers were much more attractive, with wide chimneys and steep sloping roofs curving gracefully over little verandahs. The walls were either thick gray stone or white frame, with wooden shutters painted brilliant blue or red.

At some point George lived apart from his family for one year in La Prairie:

"There was one Steve Burdow who wanted me to stay with him until I was twenty-one, and then set me up in business. He wanted me to tend store at the halfway house. It was a great place for the Canadians, who would often stop as they went to and fro between Lappery [La Prairie] and Sinyons [St. John's] to get their meals and rum, and sometimes stay all night. Had to learn the French language, and I wanted to acquire it very much. Stayed one year at the place, and then Mr. Burdow took me home. Went to school for a while."

Many of the people George waited on at the store journeyed fifteen miles from St. John's, an old French fort which had originally been a Jesuit mill. He was delighted to learn how quickly he could pick up their language and understand them.

He was fascinated by their costumes, so colorful and different from the English clothing. In winter they wore moccasins, peaked fur caps, and long coats buttoned up on one side, held fast with a yellow or red worsted sash. Their leggings were made of soft leather, and they wore their hair in pigtails. Other customers included surpliced priests, fur-trimmed officers, and militiamen garbed in all kinds of costumes, from leather jerkins and coonskin caps to brass-buttoned tail coats and tall crowned hats. They must have been an exotic sight on winter evenings, gathered in the shop before a roaring fire in the great open fireplace, the flickering of homemade candles and rush lights further illuminating the spectacle.

In summer the men wore short jackets of blue home-spun, open at the neck. There were red neckcloths, buff homespun trousers, white socks with moccasins or wooden patens, and straw hats with colored ribbon. The women wore blue or gray jackets, gay neckerchiefs in flow-ered materials, and yellow skirts with red stripes. Their tall crowned hats were of straw, like their husbands', but with a front brim.

George recalled a lightning storm striking Montreal and the surrounding territory in 1833. Since it happened during the year he worked at the shop in La Prairie, and since in any case the Hawkins family was already long es-tablished in Vermont by 1833, he may have been mistaken about the date. Quite likely he was describing the great storm that history books record as having taken place in Montreal on November 9, 1819, when George was thirteen and a half years old.

The whole morning and early afternoon had been un-usually dark. About 3 P.M., blue lightning began forking in the northwest in a rapid succession of flash and approach. Finally one remarkably vivid flash like a meteor was succeeded by an incredibly loud clap of thunder.

All the Catholics thought destruction was near, and rushed to church, where High Mass was recited, amidst candles and flower-decked saints.

Lightning struck the bell tower, and oddly enough, it was the only place it struck. Black rain fell in torrents on the late arrivals, who surrounded the church, unable to fit inside. English seamen begged permission to put out the fire, but weren't let inside for some time. When they finally succeeded in dousing the fire, they were paid about ten dollars for their labor. Many people who could afford to cross the St. Lawrence did so, to escape the disaster that they were sure was on the way.

George described his experience of the storm:

"I was standing one day after dinner and it began to turn dark all at once. Chickens began to crow, and a tongue of lightning flashed forth and shook the house. It was so near it made me reel. I had returned to the store again at this time. The owner was away to the city for more goods, and when he returned he said the Roman Church was struck and the gilded ball burnt off. Fire broke out, and was soon put down. I was much too frightened to sleep there. The master had what he called a cricket bed for himself."

From the bits and pieces of anecdotes describing George's boyhood thus far, one gathers it was not only a colorful and possibly painful one, but one which promoted a certain feistiness of spirit. This quality was apparent in George's early recollection of an incident which took place before he left England:

"Once, in England, I was going along the side of the hedge fence. The hedges there are very wide and compact. A little bird flew into it and I began to throw stones and killed it. But oh, how sorry I was afterwards!"

Some years later when George's father came to visit him at La Prairie, he had a similar impulsive and passionate outburst.

"Pa came out to see me, and brought a New Testament. I wanted to go back with him. When he would not let me go, I got mad and cut the book up. Was very sorry after I saw what I had done. Then I caught the cat and put some tobacco down her throat and watched her mew. It was fun for me then, but death for pussy. I felt badly for it afterwards and declared I would never do it again."

It seems to be around this time that George's father was finding work in Vermont, and he probably began to appreciate the idea of moving his family there. Abigail's family ties in South Hero, Vermont, no doubt encouraged those thoughts. George continued:

"Ma wanted to go and see her sister in the States, and I wanted to accompany her. Father promised me I could if I would split all the wood in the shed. In doing this I mashed my fore-finger and had to go to the doctor with it. Pa, Ma, and myself finally went, leaving my two sisters behind with his [William's] cousin. While we were away my father broke his leg, and one of my sisters took very sick.

"We were looking up a location. He [William] finally bought and done very well for a while, until sickness took him off. He died with dropsy. The family were all there. He called for me; as he was giving me his blessing, the angels seemed around his bed, and thus he passed away. God rest his soul."

But George jumped ahead of himself here, for the narration continues with the story of the family's move to Vermont, and the continuation of their life there. William, being an accomplished mason, found himself much in demand, and didn't pass away for another twenty-five or twenty-six years.

Village Life:
South Hero, Vermont

IN MID-WINTER OF 1821 the Hawkins family decided to move to South Hero, Vermont, a lively and growing town on Grand Isle in Lake Champlain. Founded in Revolutionary times, South Hero was well established, with more newspapers published there per capita than in any other town in the state; but relative to Montreal, the lake and surrounding land were still primitive and much as they had been for hundreds of years.

The sleigh that the Hawkins family took from Montreal as far as La Prairie was a carriage without wheels, with open sides ornamented with a kind of curtain. Four excellent horses drew them the entire distance in an hour and twenty minutes.

They drove through stupendous mountains of ice and chasms of wintry desolation. Though novel, the extreme cold rendered this winter ride over the river and lake rough and unpleasant. The family wrapped up snugly in buffalo skin robes and sealskin caps to keep out the piercing wind.

Deciding to make the journey without stopovers, they changed at St. John's to a horse and cutter for the night lake crossing, which they did make safely in spite of George's fears.

He briefly described the family's crossing of Lake Champlain.

"We moved to Vermont, and on the journey had to travel for a number of miles on the ice. Pa took the track. As it was dark and snowing he could not see the bushes.

He saw a light and steered for it right across the lake.

"Three times the horse stuck his hoof through the ice. The moon began to shine and I could see the ice bend. I thought if the horse and cutter went down I'd swim or scoot out on the ice. We got a man next morning to pilot us who told us the lake had just frozen over the night before, and there were many teams at the bottom of the lake."

When the Hawkins family first arrived in South Hero, it was a village of about seven hundred people, located at one end of a large island in the middle of Lake Champlain, twenty-two miles below the Canadian border, between New York and Vermont. Steamboats touched regularly at the one wharf at Gordon's Landing. Other means of lake transportation included dug-out canoes, oxen, ferries, and schooners. When the lake was frozen there were sleighs, and in the dry season one could "travel by sandbar" to mainland Vermont.

In the spring, water rose four to six feet over the sandbar, and formed about two miles of marshland on the Vermont shore at the far end of the bar.

The town spread out over several square miles to the southeast, with another population center around Keeler's Bay to the north. Outbuildings and pastures surrounded the houses, for the isle was more open than other parts of Vermont. Public buildings included a frame hotel, several schools, the Robinson store, a library, and a tannery on Keeler Bay. The two hundred and fifty "gray-paper" or leather-backed volumes in the library included neither works of fiction nor religion. The former were considered immoral, while the latter were too controversial. Nonetheless, the Methodist circuit rider included South Hero in his rounds, meeting with people in their individual homes. Congregational services were held in a schoolhouse near the sandbar, while Union services took place in the Town Hall, after it was built in 1823.

Though today's residents deny it, some historians say South Hero was the most intemperate town in the county.

To continue with George's reminiscences:

"I love to skate. I have skated fifty miles at a time, and like it better than any other amusement . . .

"William Fewster lived only about six miles from Lake Champlain. His father was the one Pa sold to. The land was one hundred acres joining Fewster, but Father never got a cent for it. The man Fewster was a cheat. He was a glassier by trade.

"No one but he and his wife and the boy in the family. In this case she was the worse half instead of the better, and she was strong enough to take him by the coat tail and throw him over the fence. They were both English. He drank rum and spent a good deal.

"He took a fancy to me, and got me to go to shambles [the meat market] when he was in Montreal, with dog and sled, carrying pork and mutton. I tended the stall.

"One day a fine looking lady came along, looked at butter, tried it. I had a quarter of mutton in the shop then, and while I was weighing the butter, with my back turned to her, she stole my mutton. I ran across the shambles, but she was gone. I didn't but hope to get a scolding about it, but my master just laughed about it. The woman had on a cloak and talked so fine, but I watched after that and didn't have any more such customers."

The shambles was part of a damp and unpleasant hollow, located in the old French market down by the river front on Craig Street. Hucksters were not allowed to sell fly-blown meat, tainted fish, or any veal past three weeks old, nor were they allowed to sell their meat anywhere out-side of the shambles. George's duties in the meat market lasted only one season.

"I didn't go [to the shambles] when storming," he con-tinued, "only a short spell one winter. I took my dog, he wagged his tail and away we went with the load. He was a nice looking dog, black, named Bateau, and I had to talk French to him."

A smart sled dog could fill the woodbox on command, fetch shoes, open a door, hunt, fetch shot game from the water, and watch the house at night. He never tired in a blizzard and could pull eighty or ninety miles a day over frozen lakes. He was trained not to chew harness or shoes when hungry and slept at his master's back at night to keep him warm.

The dog sled was made of thick oak, about fifteen inches wide and ten or twelve feet long. The front end turned up like a skate, and the sides and back were made of parchment drawn tightly around the framework and hinged so that they gave a little in collisions. The sled was very light, springy and bouncy, with the rider sitting on a comfortable, low seat, his legs tucked under blankets.

The harness, which was attached to Bateau's shoul-ders, had several small bells fastened on to it, which fitted under the dog's jaws. George yelled "Marché!" to make him go on, and other calls he used were "Yee!" and "Chough!" He evidently named the big dog "Bateau," or boat, because he could pull the loaded sled so swiftly and easily over the frozen water.

George continued:

"Well, after we came to Vermont, there was a new leaf turned over, and I went to work in earnest, tending the home place and going three miles to school in winter. In the winter evenings I would do the chores and sometimes go to a husking or parsing bee. They would string the apples there. Well, we had sport all the time, work and play, old and young, all young together."

As early as 1821 Vermont schools compared well with others in the country. The first normal school in the country was organized only a few years later in this state, and the first blackboard was invented by the school's founder. School attendance was compulsory in Vermont, and until 1826 education was financed by both voluntary subscription and local taxation. For any schooling past the primary grades, students usually paid about twenty dollars per quarter year.

In South Hero, boys went to school during the three winter months, six days a week, six hours a day. Each Monday, one hour tests were given at midday; on Friday afternoons there were special programs; and Saturdays were devoted to the study of the catechism. All study was necessarily pious, since all the textbooks, such as they were, were filled with moral precepts. Most students used their parents' old books, or had none.

Teaching often had to be by rote, since there were no blackboards, textbooks, or slates. Multiplication tables, for instance, were learned by reciting or singing them in unison, as shown in the following excerpt from *The Golden Wreath*, by L. C. Emerson, published in 1857 in Boston.

Lessons were taught from the Bible, the Psalter, and some came from Webster's *Selections*, which was a reader. There were lessons in spelling, accenting, reading English, writing, and arithmetic. Spelling was learned through daily drill, and grammar was inculcated through listening to the teacher read the rules. Grammar was also

Once 2 is 2, 2 times 2 are 4, 3 X 2 are 6, 4 X 4 are 8;
5 X 2 are 10, 6 times 2 are 12, 7 X 2 fourteen, 8 X 2, sixteen;
9 times 2, 18; 10 times 2, 20; 11 times 2, 22; 12 times 2, 24.

Chorus

5 X 5 are 25, and 6 X 5 are 30; 7 X 5 are 35, & 8 X 5 are 40; 9 X 5 are 45;

Repeat the 5-times-table after each verse, as a chorus.

10 X 5 are 50; 11 X 5 are 55; & 12 X 5 are 60.

(Sung to the tune of "Yankee Doodle.)

Learning the Tables to Music

taught by parsing — writing down the place of a word in a sentence and the part of speech to which it belonged. Geography wasn't taught in 1821 since no textbook had yet been written.

Ink was made from ink powder, maple bark, and sticks of soot dissolved in vinegar. Pens were goose quills, sharpened by the teacher. Slates were not yet in common use, and pencils were too costly. Older boys often taught, saving their monthly salaries of seventeen to twenty-five dollars with the intention of continuing their own schooling. School was let out during icy and snowy weather, and started up again about sugaring-off time in the spring.

Singing school met at night, since the singing instructors had other jobs during the day. They were paid 1 shilling, 6 pence a night. The students paid about two dollars a quarter, and brought their own wood and coal.

Singers paraded around the room in a circle, with the master in the center. He would read the rules, reminding the students to pay attention to the rise and fall of the notes. Then he would distribute books for the individual parts, give directions for the pitch, sound a note, and they would all fall to. The students liked to sing fuguing tunes, because it gave them a chance to show off. "Mi-fa-sol-la" were the singing syllables. They would beat time for themselves, making up for the quality of their performance with their high enthusiasm. Sessions usually ended with a prayer.

*   *   *   *   *

In George's accounts there are old-fashioned expressions and pronunciations that are still part of our family's daily speech. Our legacy from those early Vermont days include terms such as:

"great Caesar's ghost," "how in Sam Hill," "jumpin' Jehosephat," "land o' Goshen," "what in tarnation," "a sinkin' spell," "store-boughten," "hotter n'Tophet," "contrary as an off ox," "no great shakes," "no great punkins," "pretty small potatoes," "you couldn't find your way out of a wet paper bag," "ceegar" (cigar), "Roozia" (Russia), "all the sense the law allows," "I 'druther," and "plague it."

The holdovers from England include: "calf-lick" (cowlick), "chock-full," "clap" (put a thing in place), "clean" (entirely), "coddle," "come by" (attained), "cross-patch" (peevish person), "dickens" (the deuce), "dog-cheap," "do-up" (fasten), "hot foot," "kingdom come," "lace" (beat), "lief" (just as soon), "part an' parcel," "sauce" (scold), "scuff" (nape of the neck), "snigger," "span-new," and "to rights" (proper order).

George learned new Indian terms, too: "hominy," "pecan," "no cake," "persimmon," "pone" — all of the preceding being foods the Hawkins had never known in England. Other Indian words that have long since become part of the American English language include: "toboggan," "moccasin," "papoose," "pow-wow," "moose," and "opossum."

*　*　*　*　*

George told of being punished when he was naughty:

"Once, when at school, myself and some more boys decided not to go in, but the master sent some large boys after us, and one of them took me on his back and lugged me in. In consequence of my misdeeds, I had to stand the rest of the afternoon on a bench on one foot, while the master thrashed the other two boys. One time I went and played in a pool where I was forbidden to go, took cold, got down with a fever and come near dying."

Clearly, teachers didn't hesitate to assume a stern discipline with their pupils. The rod, the dunce cap, and the whipping post were all used freely. Beech switches four or five feet long stood in the corner of the classroom, in full sight.

One gathers that in social spheres, George's manner was equally rough-and-ready, a curious blend of bluster and shyness. He continued with the following:

"I got Pa to buy me a new suit of clothes and I attended dancing school, but oh! How bashful I was at first. Soon got over it or out of it. After I got to going I found that I was up to the best of them, firm and steady always, and I always bought tickets to the entertainments whether I went or not. I did not care for the girls, but liked to be in their society, and the boys called me what is known now as a lady's man. We went to all the balls for miles around. We would be tired out and unable to go to work or school, and I would get to thinking that it was all wrong and swear off, but I kept on going just the same. I believe I had rather dance than to eat then."

According to the styles of the times, George's suit probably had long, rather loose pantaloons made of dark "kerseymore" (a woolen cloth), worn with a light waistcoat and a dark blue jacket, the latter cut longer in back than in front. He may have worn a soft bow tie at the neck.

George recollected his first trip to the fair:

"I remember that I used to get very tired at home working and walking, but one day Pa took us, me and my sisters, to the fair and I did not get tired that day, as it was something we had not yet seen. That was the first time I had seen any drunkenness. There, well-dressed men were drunk and spewing around, while I could not bear the smell of liquor, but got used to it when I became a man."

South Hero, close to Canada and conveniently situated on a waterway leading down to the States, lay in the path of one of the greatest smuggling routes in the country. Both gambling and counterfeiting were common in the bordering county. It isn't known if William Hawkins participated in the custom of offering alcoholic refreshment to his workers when they were putting up a stone house. If so, in those days rum would have been the proffered sustenance.

The agricultural fair that George's family attended was probably the one held across the lake in Plattsburg, New York. In 1824, this annual fair was described as being held in an open meadow, with a showing of bulls, cows, calves, oxen, horses, pigs, and sheep. A platform was erected under a tree for exhibiting women's handiwork and for the awarding of prizes. Curiously, women at first resisted showing their work, fearing that they would be criticized for appearing in public.

Other entertainments at the fair included games of hammer throwing, stone putting, jumping, and sack races. The Hawkins' saw Indian games, hockey and shinney, war and scalp dancing. There may have been Scottish hornpipe dancing, slack rope-walking, a carousel, and acrobats performing on horseback as well. Certainly there were cattle judging and horse racing, though in Vermont it became illegal to bet on horses after 1823.

Church; Farming; Masonry

GEORGE HAD THIS TO say about his spiritual musings:

"Once, on a Sunday at a meeting, the minister said the spirit of God was in everything. I was in the back seat with my back against the wall, and his sentence startled me. I looked and wondered if He was in the plastering, but couldn't understand it anyway. I was scared more than once by his sermons and the talk of Hell, until I sometimes imagined I could hear the chains dragged across the floor."

While in Vermont, George retained his affiliation with the Church of England. Later on in his life, after moving to Indiana, he became a Methodist, until he finally joined the Christian Church at Macy, Indiana, sometime between 1875 and 1880.

The Hawkins family farmed a bit, at least enough to fulfill their own requirements. The soil on Grand Isle was rich and fertile, and up until 1820 grain was an important crop. Wheat, corn, and oats were grown as both food crops and for purposes of distilling. In 1820 the crops were ravaged by insects and the grain business was ruined for small farmers. Too, they suffered from competition from western New York.

Farmers then turned to growing fruit trees, primarily apple, but other fruits included plums, cherries, grapes, pears, currants, gooseberries, and strawberries. There was sugaring, though not as widely practiced as in the northern counties. South Hero was generally level, with occasional hills and small tracts of rolling land, and a good deal more forest was present then than there is now. A sawmill operated part of the year; and leather, potash, and pearlash were all manufactured products of the region.

Farmers also began raising merino sheep and cattle, and certainly the Hawkins family was no exception. They kept cattle for butter, cheese, milk, and beef, and eventually obtained leather for shoes, harnesses, and buckets.

Their sheep supplied them with wool and mutton, and made it possible for the Hawkins family to produce much of their own clothing as well. As was typical of most families in rural areas back then, Abigail spun her own wool, and she may have had another spinning wheel for producing linen as well. Not every home had a loom, but with our people, ever since those early days weaving has always been a family tradition, handed down from mother to daughter. Indeed, there were several Hawkins handwoven coverlets still being used in my home when I was growing up. In every generation up until the present there has been at least one weaver in the family, and right now I know of three of them.

* * * * *

The time came when George decided to take up his father's trade:

"After staying at home, and plowing and hoeing and working on the farm, Pa wanted to know the trade I would like to follow. I wanted at first to be a sailor, but Pa said it took nine of them to make a man, so I got out of that notion.

"Well, I was to be a mason, and began carrying stone for an Irishman, for the construction of a fine stone store;

I carried them on a hand barrow. We had shoulder straps to slip on the shoulder; he went first, me behind. As I was stout then, he liked to see me lift. But I got sick and had to take my bed, and was so weak I could not move for a while, and was weakened for life.

"Afterwards, in Indiana, when I had a job of plastering, my wrist got so weak I was unable to shove the trowel along, and I had to quit and get help. I waited until I got the use of myself, and then went back with two men and finished the job. . . "

Though George liked to give the impression that he was sickly and accident-prone, the fact remains that he learned his craft from his father who was a master stone-mason. William taught his son how to work slate, do brick work, and lay stone walls that were the pride of South Hero. Stonework there was better than that done in the Berkshires or the Catskills, with both better stone and better workmanship.

There were three quarries in South Hero, as well as a brickyard at the mouth of the Lamoille River. Mortar, col-ored dark tan and often decorated with a distinctive brush line of white, was made of native lime, according to a zealously guarded secret formula. Together, this father-son team could lay walls of both strength and beauty, sometimes "knitting" the walls with stones of various sizes so that no mortar was necessary to secure them. Later and elsewhere, wealthy men had their homes built of dressed marble, but in South Hero the houses were ex-ceedingly plain, of local gray or reddish limestone or marble. The typical island door was arched, wider than av-erage, with no adornment, and an extremely simple mantel. Gateposts, cornerposts, and foundations were all of undressed granite.

To this day there stands the Benajah Phelps house, also known as the Phelps-Reade house, as testimony to the fine craftsmanship that William Hawkins brought to his work. With the help of the two oldest Phelps boys, he built this house in the year 1817 in just sixty-three days. This record-breaking speed was even documented in the town's official historical records. The house has three fine fireplaces; the one in the kitchen is equipped with a brick oven.

In the dust loft of one end of a finishing shed, William sat in his office and did his book work, making every stone and every man hour of work count. It took about five months to build a stone house, costing its owner anywhere from twelve to fifteen hundred dollars.

Quarrying, an industry which started in America shortly after the War of 1812, was an important business on the island, where stone cost about eight dollars a foot. Stone bridges, so common in England, were rare in the new country, and the early stone was used primarily for millstones, doorsteps, posts, and window lintels. Stone-cutting was hazardous, requiring extreme skill, and was considered well-paid work by the standards of the day.

The quarries were ridged holes, stairstepping down and down, with homemade ladders reaching from one ledge to another. There was usually water standing at the bottom. Ropes were used to haul up the stone, which was in turn taken away on carts and sleighs, usually in the winter. In spring and summer when roads were muddy, an eight-horse team was not enough to haul the stones, and three to five such teams were then necessary. In winter the ice made the hills too fast, so clog chains were used on the runners to slow them down in steep places. A twenty-five-mile trip took about eighteen hours and brought in about four dollars' pay.

In South Hero, walls were usually laid in the summer, at fifty cents a rod. A man and his oxen usually made about one dollar a day for backbreaking work.

* * * * *

During this period when the Hawkins family were establishing their new life on Grand Isle, Abigail and William continued to expand their family, in the end giving George a total of ten half brothers and sisters. George was twelve when William, Jr. was born in 1818, and twenty-three when the last child, Jemima, was born in 1839. His stepmother was undoubtedly caught up with her babies and housework, and it is unlikely that George felt close home ties at this time of his life. There is no specific date to attach to the following reminiscence:

"Once, when I began to think of doing for myself, I collected all my money, and started to seek my fortune alone. I started on foot, and the first day got very tired— stayed all night at a farm house — supper, bed and breakfast was fifty cents, but I slept very sound. . . .

"As I had heard they wanted masons in Lowell [Massachusetts], I took the stage for that place. My first dinner on the stage journey cost fifty cents, and I had hardly more than set down when the stage drove up to the door and the driver sung out, 'All aboard.' When I got to Lowell, I rubbed my face all over with a brick to harden myself a little more. I got into work right away, at the rate of two dollars a day."

George told about another trip to Boston:

"A chum of mine one day asked me as we were going to dinner if I would like to buy a lottery ticket; he had two and would sell me one for two dollars. I traded him a watch for one, and his ticket was a blank and mine drew thirty dollars. I drew my money, went to Boston, worked around a little and made more money, then went home to spend the winter as there was nothing doing there."

Back home, George had an accident, and ruined his new boot:

"Once, when in Vermont, I had on my first new pair of boots and was in the woods chopping. Guess I must have been thinking of something else, for all at once I felt the blade going into my foot. I looked around for the piece of boot and then went home. They had a hard time to stop the flow of blood. But I did not care so much for that as for the boot, for I knew it would look bad when mended.

"Father had to go to the woods then or hire a hand. He was no hand at chopping, had never learned. He could use a mallet and chisel, though, and was a capital hand at dressing stone, of which he did a great deal in England. I heard him say a short time after coming to America he wished he was back in England, as times were so dull."

It's hard to imagine how William found the time to be bored with his life, with a house full of children on the one hand, and his skilled work being in such high demand on the other. However, these are George's stories. Unfortunately, William left behind no written record which might have given an impression of his own personality, and more significantly, an idea of how an English immigrant of the early 1800s felt about bringing his family to the New World, almost immediately losing his first wife, and then starting fresh.

However, George's voice captures a lot on its own. One can appreciate the degree of effort it took for early settlers to adapt to new ways, and to carve out new lives in a land which was largely "unformed," compared to the European standards that they had left behind.

Largesse on Lake and Island

ONCE, IN AN ELDERHOSTEL class on family history, I tried to tell about the rich natural resources on Grand Isle, Vermont, in the early 1880s.

"Why, a horse once had it's leg broken by the swarm of fish in a stream it tried to cross," I said.

"You're crazy! Fish breaking a horse's leg! Preposterous!" they hooted at me.

Though it really is almost impossible to believe such stories, an overwhelming abundance of resources existed in 1821 or 1822, when the family moved from Montreal to Grand Isle in Lake Champlain, Vermont. Fifteen hundred pounds of salmon were taken at one haul of the seine at Chesterfield, and they were so thick at Plattsburg that it was truly dangerous to ride a spirited horse across the stream. Lake fish included black bass, pickerel, muskellunge, wall-eyed pike, yellow perch, trout, whitefish, and silvery chub. Settlers were astonished at the plenty of fish, game, and native verdure that were found at that time. Bears were so numerous that they were seen almost daily. On Grand Isle there were also wolves, lynx, catamounts, and beavers.

Crows were so common that a three-cent bounty was offered for each one of them. There were wild geese, ducks, seagulls, and pigeons by the thousands — twenty-five pigeon nests could be found in a single tree. Hundreds of acres of such trees grew everywhere, and the ground around them was covered with two inches of droppings. Squabs, gathered by cutting down a tree, were loaded on a horse in a few minutes' time.

Grand Isle, a low, densely forested island, overlooked four miles of island-dotted water. A few small springs, useful to grass-eating wild and domestic animals for their salt content, were also said to be good for man's chronic complaints and skin diseases, mainly because of their high iodine content.

There were elms and poplars, very large and hundreds of years old. Every year along the lake front a few were washed away by ice and waves. The island, which was a little hilly, boasted on its fifteen square miles much more open pastureland than settlers found in other parts of the state.

South Hero quarries were primarily shale and limestone (rather than granite or marble). The limestone was of three types. Fine blue-grey limestone was quarried on the south shore and was used in rough masonry. The nearly black Trenton limestone came from the western part of town near the lake, running north and south. This type, called firestone, stood fire very well and was used for fireplaces. Isle LaMotte limestone was black and fine-grained and came from the middle of the east side of the island. This stone took a high polish, was very durable, and though hard to work it was used often.

The richest marble deposit in the world was found along the eastern shore of the lake, in forty shades from black to white, including blue, grey, rose, pink, sapphire, mottled, veined, and composite.

On to the West

THIS IS A STORY that chokes me up no matter how many times I tell it. There weren't any social services in George's time, just people loving people, including strangers, and giving a free impartial hand to one another. Perhaps it's best to let George tell it in his own words:

"Several of the boys whom I knew were getting married and I concluded to pop the question to my best girl. Her father was dead, but three brothers were living. I hardly knew how to get at it, but finally made up my mind and waded through a snow storm one night to her home, and we were soon married."

So George married Abigail Jane Davidson on a cold day in February, in the year 1834. Abigail was his junior by nine years. Not very romantic so far, but at least a snow storm made it memorable. Their first son, of what was to be a family of eight children, was born in March of the following year. They named him Thomas W. Hawkins.

George continued:

"The boys [Abigail's three Davidson brothers] and I decided to work together. . . . The following summer I made four hundred and fifty dollars clear of all expenses. I bought a piece of land and some small property, moved on it and lived there until I moved to Indiana. I also bought what was considered the best span of horses in the town, or anywhere around there.

"We started for Indiana [George, Abigail, their son, Abigail's mother and her three brothers] with double sleigh, sold it and bought a wagon, stopped on the way by very muddy and foul weather. We stayed through the

44

summer and left again in the fall.

"Shortly after this I took very sick, got out of my mind and the wrong medicine they gave me came very near finishing me. I had the lock-jaw along with it, and the doctor came and forced something down me which finally brought me out all right. But it was a very close call.

"I did not want to die and leave my family in their destitute circumstances. Well, as that country seemed to me to be almost wilderness, I concluded I could not live there anymore. I took down sick and was under the weather about four years. When I recovered everything was gone but my trade. Winter came on — and no wood at the door and no pay for anyone."

George was a master mason, fortunate to have studied masonry with his father on Grand Isle, a rock-bound terrain rich in the finest quality stone. However, in the forested wilderness where they were forced to stop when George became ill, stone fences and houses were not in great demand. By this time, Abigail's mother and brothers had gone on, pushing ahead to their destination in Indiana, though the mother died along the way and was buried at an unknown spot in the wilderness.

So the Hawkins family, separated from the Davidsons, now found themselves hundreds of miles from the nearest family and friends.

George went on:

"The neighbors, hardworking, jolly good fellows, came and helped me out. One morning I found a large pile of wood at the door. The best medicine I took of any that winter, and the next spring I felt like a new man.

"I told a man I worked for, a Mr. Rose, that I'd been going through the mill, and hadn't got over the effects of it yet. Under his direction I continued doctoring, and dog-

45

wood bitters and quinine brought me through. I think we must have used a barrel of the bitters, and we bought the quinine by the ounce. [Dogwood bitters are an antacid folk remedy for heartburn.]

"When I started for Indiana it was to do better for me and the family. It was a with a heavy heart that I left, as all of our family was in tears. But we got along and did very well after all. I have learned one lesson in my lifetime and that is never look back."

There may be hundreds of versions of this same story — the pioneer stories of people who had yet to put down their permanent roots. Folks come together by chance, lightly touching each others' lives with the mutual care and concern that the bare bones of hard living inspire. Then they separate and move on, each man or woman going on to complete his or her own story — sad at the parting, but always wishing each other well, demonstrating the inherent goodness of all human beings.

Tecumseh's Last Raid

IN 1795, TWENTY-ONE YEARS before the Hawkins family began their new life in Canada, another branch of our family, the Mulhollands, emigrated to the New World from Ireland. The Mulhollands were a substantial family, who owned the famous linen mills in Belfast mentioned by Dickens in one of his novels.

Leaving his family behind, John Mulholland immediately returned to his native land, where he met a pretty young woman named Isabel, right there in the Irish port. Isabel herself was bound for America. In the course of questioning John about the new land, she was told she had better look up his sons and marry one of them.

Isabel went to America. It came to pass that one day Isabel was out riding in Painted Post, New York and at the end of her trot a fine young man helped her off her horse. He was none other than Daniel, son of John, and sure enough, the two were wed shortly thereafter, in 1795.

In 1806 Daniel moved his family to what was then called Frenchtown, presently known as Monroe, Michigan, situated on the River Raisin. This proved to be the site of Tecumseh's Last Raid.

Chief Tecumseh of the Shawnees, charismatic leader of all the Eastern Indian Tribes, had resolved to regain the hunting grounds of the Indians, and to this end had contrived to be made a brigadier general in the British army during the War of 1812. Tecumseh did not know, of course, that in doing so he had allied himself and his people with the soon-to-be-vanquished opposition.

On January twenty-second, 1813, Daniel and Isabel Mulholland, along with their nine children, found themselves hiding in their attic, covering their ears so they couldn't hear the crashes and savage yelps taking place down below, as the British and the Indians looted the Mulholland's home. Daniel was carried off as a prisoner, in what came to be known as the River Raisin Massacre.

Later on, the children were so distraught at the sight of so many bodies killed in battle throughout the town that Isabel sought refuge with friends on a nearby farm, and it was there that Daniel found them after he was released. He had heard that Chief Tecumseh, leader of the raid, had been killed, but nonetheless felt that the family would be safer if they found some means to escape the area until peace was made with the Indians.

To this end, the family boarded an abandoned raft found on the shore of Lake Erie, and though the raft had no oars, the Mulhollands improvised with poles, and pushed off into the cold October waters.

Thus they drifted for several days across Lake Erie, no doubt haunted by vivid scenes of their home and outbuildings burning, their belongings stolen and destroyed. Isabel held the family tea pot on her lap, and when she once sighted a small bonfire on shore, she saw it as a chance to boil water for tea and insisted that they land. Debarking, they found ribbons scattered nearby which they recognized as having been stolen from their clothesline by the raiding Indians back in Frenchtown. They left in a hurry, without their tea.

The cold, frightened family finally landed just west of Cleveland, Ohio, where Daniel found work on a farm. He kept Isabel and the younger children with him, but the older two were "bound out" to work for their room and board. Eventually, Daniel bought a team and wagon and took the reunited family back to Monroe, where they resettled on government land on the south bank of the Raisin River.

Blind Fate

ELIZABETH CLASPED THE note from her husband to her bosom. Samuel wanted her to visit him! She missed him dreadfully; she would hurry down the lane right away to hire a wagon, make arrangements for boating out to the lighthouse, and soon be reunited with her husband.

Samuel Day Choate, grandfather of my great-grandmother, Sarah Ann Mulholland, lived alone in the Turtle Island Lighthouse, after being appointed its keeper. He had been a member of a cavalry troop in the Revolutionary War, and was a hatter by trade. Earlier in their marriage, the couple had lived on the river Thames in Moraviantown, Ontario, close to Elizabeth's father, a Loyalist to the Crown who had moved to Canada from Danbury, Connecticut. On February 17, 1816, just after the close of the French and Indian War, Samuel and Elizabeth moved to Frenchtown (Monroe, Michigan) from Ohio, where they had lived for nine years. And now, after seven happy years in Frenchtown, for Samuel there was the added thrill of a new job with fresh new responsibilities. The lighthouse, which was constructed in 1821, had a fifty-five foot tower and was equipped with eleven lights.

Elizabeth vividly remembered their excitement at moving back to the States. Living in Frenchtown, the site of Tecumseh's last raid on the River Raisin, was far more to her liking than life had been in either Canada or Ohio. And no doubt there was a romantic appeal for Samuel, to be the sole keeper of a lighthouse, sometimes visited by his adoring wife.

What fun for Elizabeth to have some time with him

there! She told the driver of the wagon to pick her up again in a week.

One could picture them settling down to a quiet life at last: the war was over, Elizabeth had a new home to furnish, Samuel had a new job much to his liking. But it did not happen that way. In the year of 1823, cholera was one of the most dreaded of all diseases. It ran its fatal course swiftly, with the patient often dying within three to five days of its inception.

Elizabeth arrived at the lighthouse and found her husband already weak and burning with fever. Perhaps he had caught it from flies. She wept over his body, and prepared it for burial. It was a week before someone came to take her home.

A Plethora of Preachers

OF ALL THE PREACHERS on both my mother's and father's sides of the family, Joseph Carter (1786–1849), my father's great-grandfather, probably had the roughest life. In *The Backwoods Preacher,* Peter Cartwright gives us an idea of a preacher's life in those times:

"I think I received about eighty dollars the whole year of 1806. . . . Those were hard times in the Western wilds. In that early day many preachers did not receive in a whole year money enough to get them a suit of clothes. If preachers had not dressed in homespun clothing, and the good sisters had not made and presented them with clothing, they must leave the itinerant life, go to work, and clothe themselves."* In referring to Joseph Carter, Cartwright had this to say:

"He was a powerful speaker. Once when a camp meeting was about to be deluged by a heavy thunder storm, Carter prayed away the clouds and saved the day, with sunshine coming down directly on his pulpit, like a benison from heaven."**

Carter's circuit extended along the Mississippi River from present day Nauvoo, Illinois all the way to Hannibal, Missouri. He covered the area on horseback, riding with a rifle across his pommel. At night he was obliged to sleep on dirt floors in rustic cabins provided by the pioneer

---

* Peter Cartwright, *Autobiography of Peter Cartwright: The Backwoods Preacher* (New York :Hunt & Eaton, 1856).
**Ibid.

My great-grandfather, Charles Eagy, a Methodist preacher

farmers. For pay he received room and board, and sometimes one or two suits of clothes in the course of a year.
The old man who had married Joseph to his wife Susan-
nah Wiley years before, later remarked that Carter was a
well-educated man, and wondered why he went into such
a hard life "except that he was called into it." This is what
Grandpa Eli Carter told us.

Rushville, Indiana, was the Carter family seat, and it
was there that a J. Carter was appointed preacher at
Balls Chapel Methodist Episcopal Church in 1832, the
year after it was founded. The name was then changed to
Carter Chapel. My father's other grandfather, Charles
Eagy, was also a Methodist preacher. My great-great-
grandfather John Mulholland, of Monroe, Michigan, held
the first Methodist services in his home.

But not all the preachers in our family were Methodist.
Though my mother's ancestors were Irish, there have not
been many who were raised as Catholics, and this is for
an amusing reason. All the sons of Ireland married
strong-minded Scotch-Presbyterians from North Ireland,
who saw to it that their husbands became Protestant.

There was one noted exception. My grandfather Harry
Keegan's favorite aunt, Margaret Keegan O' Brien, was
widowed and left with three children to raise. One son
died at a young age, but the other, Monsignor Frank
O'Brien (1851–1921), became a famous prelate in Kalamazoo, Michigan. His name is still honored there, for he
founded eight of the early Catholic institutions in Kalamazoo, and was subsequently called "one of the greatest
parish priests in the United States." He served the people
of Kalamazoo for forty years, and when he died, his parish
in St. Augustine was the third largest in the country.

Top: Msg.. Frank O'Brien, cousin
(1831– 1921), Kalamazoo, Michigan

Bottom: Suella Weiland Henn,
niece, hospital Chaplain on Long
Island, New York

He was a man of extraordinary gifts. It was once said of him that had he rather chosen to pursue a worldly career, he would have been one of the greatest statesmen of his time. Besides his parish work he studied and wrote about the history of Michigan, published a number of books, served on the board of the West Point Military Academy, and was a lecturer at the University of Michigan. He had a degree and also honorary law degrees from the University of Michigan and Notre Dame University.

Growing up, he was a gentle, lovable boy, possessed a sparkling wit, and later on in life never allowed others to serve him. His sister, Mary Raphael, a nun and a medical doctor, called him a "ninny" for preaching and practicing the policy of turning the other cheek.

He probably would have been amused by an incident that occurred in our neighborhood when we were very young. We were all Protestant families, and we children were quarreling among ourselves one day, Baptist against Methodist, disputing some Catholic practice or doctrine that none of us knew beans about. And since there was total ignorance on all sides, the "debate" could progress nowhere until finally I heatedly declared:

"Well, I ought to know since I'm directly descended from a Catholic priest!"

I thereby settled the argument and was conceded victor of the debate, just by vaguely remembering there was a Catholic priest somewhere in the family.

My niece, Suella Weiland Henn, recently converted to Catholicism, and then decided she wanted to become a priest.

"Never mind," she answered the people who told her that would be impossible. Said Suella, "Someday there will be women priests in the Church, and I will be ready."

She had been raised as a Methodist, and earlier in the course of her married life she taught biochemistry. Once her children were grown and gone, Suella entered a seminary and took all but one of the courses; that is, a course that was offered to priests only.

Upon graduating, Suella became a hospital chaplain, and since then has received recognition in the local community for her work with groups and individuals in teaching them how to deal with grief.

Ellen's Beau,
George Armstrong Custer

The BOY TURNED HIS cousin's sword back and forth to catch the sunlight on its shining surface. The year was 1848, the place New Rumley, Ohio, and the sword had served its owner in the Mexican war. The boy, George Armstrong Custer, was nine years old, and already he looked forward to the glamour of a soldier's life. His manner of play already showed the cocky and rambunctious nature of a man who would play a large part in contributing to the devastation of the Indian people. He knew even then that the military life would suit him best.

Custer attended West Point, the United States Military Academy, graduating in 1861 at the bottom of his class. A few years later he reversed his "last place" rank by winning fame as a fearless cavalry leader in the Battle of Bull Run, during the Civil War.

Great things were happening in the world, and Custer fancied that he would be part of them. His life was short, but his dream did come true, for he did achieve a kind of notoriety in the history of nineteenth-century America.

On furlough in the winter of 1863, Custer visited his sister in Monroe, Michigan. One day he asked her about the two beautiful sisters he had met at her home.

"Oh, Ellen and Amelia Mulholland — Ellen is a year older than you, Amelia a year younger. They're the prettiest and most popular girls in town, the grand-daughters of one of Monroe's founders, Daniel Mulholland. The story goes that he and his family were burned out of their home during Tecumseh's last raid here on the River Raisin, in the French and Indian wars."

"Ellen is the prettiest; I'm going to marry her," Custer announced confidently. His sister laughed.

"Stand in line, George. You may have a chance," she replied.

Custer courted Ellen, proposed marriage, and was turned down. She was amused by this blustering upstart, a raw, awkward, country youth, and decided he was just what her shy girlfriend Libby needed. So Ellen introduced him to Elizabeth Bacon, a woman who would prove to be a well-suited complement to her husband's exaggerated sense of himself.

Later, when Custer returned to Monroe the following autumn on a twenty-day leave, he was recovering from a flesh wound, which he had received in the course of serving brilliantly as aide-de-camp to General McClellan. At the time, Sheridan considered Custer to be one of the greatest cavalry leaders of the war. Swaggering with that kind of confidence, Custer proposed to Libby during that furlough, and she accepted. He went back to duty, and when he returned to Monroe in February of 1864 he and Libby were wed. Custer was twenty-five years old.

Throughout the entire thirteen years of their marriage Libby stayed by Custer's side, the only "army wife" to do so, regardless of their living accommodations. Sometimes "home" was a leaky tent, sometimes an isolated cabin, sometimes officers' quarters, and sometimes a shelter in the middle of a prairie, where soldiers stumbled in to find protection from the cold. Libby followed her husband wherever he was posted, traveling from fort to fort by wagon, steamer, and train.

The Custers lived in Washington D.C., Texas, Michigan, Kansas, Kentucky, the Dakotas, and Montana.

Custer loved each move passionately, and Libby presumably matched his enthusiasm with her own. Libby's book, *Boots and Saddles: My Life in Dakota with General Custer*, is a fascinating account of their daily life in camp and fort in the West.

Custer distinguished himself as head of the Michigan cavalry brigade at Gettysburg. In November of 1868 he served under Hancock against the Cheyenne Indians in Kansas, where the troops were badly beaten at the Washita River. Custer wrote articles for magazines, and published a book in 1875 entitled, *My Life on the Plains*. His men either loved or hated him, sometimes labeling him, "Glory Hunter."

Libby also published *Tenting on the Plains* and *Following the Guidon*. In both works she spoke only of how her husband was lionized, never of how he was loathed.

In 1876 he was commissioned to find an Indian village in Montana Territory, and so confident was Custer that his six hundred and fifty men could easily vanquish this small pocket of the "enemy" that he booked a speaking tour back East in advance of his expected triumph.

Custer divided his regiment into three columns, anticipating a certain victory over only one thousand Indians. However, he had been misinformed. There were in fact between fifteen hundred and three thousand Indians in the village: Custer's men never stood a chance. The Lakota Sioux and Cheyenne Indians, led by chiefs Two Moon and Crazy Horse, brought about Custer's downfall. In 1876 he died in battle at the age of thirty-seven, without progeny.

Controversy about this battle continues to this day; Custer has been both supported and attacked. Supporters think of the battle as an heroic effort and call it "Custer's Last Stand." Today's native Americans call it the

"Battle of the Little Bighorn," and remind historians that their ancestors were fighting for their homeland, that it was a last brave stand of a culture against extermination. The Crow Indians are the tribal residents in the area to-day.

During a television show entitled "Last Stand at Little Big Horn," written by James Welch, narrator Pulitzer Prize winner M. Scott-Momaday pointed out that General William Sherman himself had warned the Indians that white men should be stopped before they killed all the Indians.

My cousin Ellen Mulholland, courted left and right throughout the town, did finally marry a soldier herself, though her choice of husband was apparently a more thoughtfully considered one.

Home in Indiana

THE HAWKINS FAMILY established themselves on their homestead in Indiana in the 1840s and 1850s. A description of their life would be in stark contrast to that of other family members who were among the first white people to settle in Indian Territory, before and after the first Land Run of 1891. Both were pioneer ways of living, but they had little or nothing in common at first. George Hawkins was a master builder in stone, wood, and brick. Consequently, the usual roughly hewn "make-do" shelter that most pioneers put up with would never have satisfied his standards. He was too much of a craftsman.

George's autobiography did not continue long enough to include his Indiana experiences, but letters and interviews with other family members give rich detail. The journey from Vermont seemed endless but in 1837 Great Grandpa George Hawkins finally arrived with his family, and began settling on a homestead not too far from Macy, Indiana. It was one hundred and sixty acres of virgin land, rich and timbered, and George immediately began building the family home and tilling their fields.

The construction of the house went on until 1856, and the facts indicate that it was a highly skilled labor of love indeed. It was the first brick house in the county, and George burned those bricks himself, from clay that he found on his own land. He cut timber from his own walnut groves, and thus provided his home with a clapboard roof, as well as wooden trim.

"That walnut woodwork must have been beautiful," I commented to Grandma Ida Keegan, youngest of the

The Hawkins family farm in Indiana. Great-Grandmother and Great-Grandfather Jane and George Hawkins stand to the right; Grandmother Ida shows off her beautiful dress on the porch to the left.

ten children raised in the house.

"Oh, we didn't like the markings to show on the wood," she protested, "so we painted all the woodwork. But those shingles lasted without replacement or repair for the life of the house, until it was torn down in 1918."

Cosette Patrick, my grandmother's niece, used to be sent to the farm for most vacations and holidays, sometimes staying there for several weeks during the summer. She and my grandmother have described a lush countryside, not far from the Wabash River, west of Fort Wayne, our Keegan bailiwick.

Great Aunt Vic, Cosette's mother, wrote that the land was all wilderness in 1837, when the Hawkins family first arrived. The Indian Trail came south from Macy on the way to Peru, Indiana, where there was a reservation across the Wabash River. The Wabash Valley was then densely timbered and level, the rich soil was without stones, the streams were clear and unfailing. Deer and small game were abundant, as were wild turkey, prairie fowl, quail, pigeons, and water fowl. Hundreds of large snakes were finally cleared out by prairie fires and wild hogs. Three million acres of federal lands were still open then for settlement, and from 1836 until 1840, George laid brick for houses and other buildings in nearby towns. Some of the rough fieldstone porches of those houses are probably still in use.

Cosette's grandmother, "Jane," was never called by her proper name, Abigail, perhaps to distinguish her from George's stepmother who bore the same name. Jane reared her own eight children in the spacious farmhouse, as well as two of her brother's children, who had lost both of their parents. Jane was reportedly nurse, doctor, and friend to all the ill and ailing for miles around. In short, she seems to have embodied the qualities of the American pioneer woman: energetic and dedicated to

*Grandmother and her brothers and sisters: Victoria
(Stratton); Ida (Keegan); Julia (Hoffman); Albert; Viola
(Patterson)—the Hawkins Family.*

the nurturing of others. In Cosette's words:

"At first they [the Hawkins] cooked in the big fireplace in the living room. Between the fireplace and front window was Grandma's corner, with her spinning wheel and a little marble-top table with the inch cactus she prized, and a charm string made of buttons, more than a yard long and hung at the right-hand corner. Buttons were traded with friends, reminders of clothing and occasions of the past, and for this reason they were cherished.

"In winter the parents slept in a double bed in an alcove near the fireplace and upstairs doorway, keeping a log fire going so nothing would freeze.

"In a side wall of the basement stairs, Grandpa kept the quinine and medicine they used. In the rock and cement basement they kept potatoes, and three big bins full of apples from one fall to the next spring. Twenty-five bee stands in the yard filled a honey dish on the table at every meal.

"The parlor was a very formal room with walnut furniture, upholstered in black mohair. I slept in the parlor bedroom where it was so cold Grandma put hot coals in the warming-pan to heat the sheets, and there was a sort of feather mattress for cover."

To this day in our home in Boise, Idaho, we still have a beautiful blue and white coverlet that Jane wove. It is woven in the Governor's Garden pattern, and we keep it in our guest room. The weaving is of such fine quality that the coverlet is still in use after a hundred years or more. The family records tell us that Jane cared for the sheep, subsequently carded, spun, and dyed the wool, and finally wove it into cloth of great beauty and utility.

Members of the family cherish other objects from that household, such as a cut glass toothpick holder, and a glass bowl with frosted lion heads composing its base, lid, and handle. This latter always stood in the middle of the

Ida Hawkins (Harry Keegan's wife), as a little girl

table, filled with apple butter at harvest time.

My grandmother, Ida, remembered the farmhouse as being the finest in the countryside. A construction man once told us it would take him five years to build such a house in the same way as George had done, with hand-fired bricks and without the use of modern tools.

The Hawkins family raised cows, horses, sheep, and geese, and made all their household linens and clothing themselves. Indeed, I remember that my great aunt Vic continued throughout her whole life to sew clothes for those of us in the next generation as well. All the girls but Grandma, the baby, were taught to spin, weave, quilt, embroider, and sew. Ida was born twenty-five years after Tom, who had died in the Civil War when she was just four years old. Being the youngest, she was likely coddled by all her siblings, and spared a lot of the more tiresome chores. As a matter of fact, neither she nor any of her daughters or granddaughters have ever been noted as good cooks!

Keegan family in Ft. Wayne, Indiana. Back row: Cosette (Mother), Charles Croll, Edith (Yarnell)), Edwin A., Mary Ann Crall, Abigail Choate. Front row: Helen, Mildred (Marsh), Margaret Ann, Patrick Henry (Great Grandpa), Kenneth, Hugh Glen.

Great-Grandmother Sarah Ann Mulholland Keegan (1831-1914) wife of Patrick Henry Keegan.

The Keegan homestead in Ft. Wayne

From Ambassador to Serf

Perhaps not too many folk have both an ambassador and a serf in their family tree, and more certainly, there must be very few indeed who can trace both such ancestors to one and the same person.

Charles Eagy, whose letter to a younger brother was quoted in the last chapter, was related through marriage to one Charles Christopher Springer (1658 – 1738), son of Lady Beata, lady companion to Queen Hedwig Eleanora of Sweden. Born and educated in Sweden, Springer was appointed by the queen as ambassador to the Court of St. James in the capital of Great Britain. In the course of carrying out his diplomatic duties in London society, it was his fate one day to be shanghaied aboard an American ship, and upon arriving in the new world, sold as a slave in Virginia.

A 1937 history of Wilmington, Delaware, tells his story:

"Going home to his lodgings [in London], late one night, he was seized by ruffians and carried on board a ship and made prisoner. He was sold to a Virginia planter and served as a redemptioner for a term of years, that is, made a servant in exchange for the cost of his passage." His indentureship lasted three years, after which time he sought out the Swedes living in Delaware and settled there with them permanently. Some details are offered from the same history quoted above:

"While there [in Virginia] he heard of a settlement of Swedes on the Delaware River and at the end of his service he joined them. Springer spared neither time nor money in behalf of his countrymen, and after the Old Swede's Church was built his name appears in church transactions as warden. He lies buried under the walls of the addition which was built in 1762, the vestry deciding it to be more respectful not to disturb his remains by removing them."

A further note about Charles appeared in *Reminiscences of Wilmington*, by Montgomery:

"There was an antique log cabin still standing in 1851, already one hundred and twenty years old, a cabin erected by Charles Springer." In fact, the Swedes are said to have introduced the log cabin to America, and according to their tradition, built their cabins out of whatever native timber was available.*

Again, from the *Reminiscences of Wilmington*:

"Among his [Springer's] descendants was an old lady who lived there who had a way with plants, a passion for flowers and the skill and taste to cultivate them successfully. She was the wife of Joseph Springer, Charles's descendent; they had no children, and had many orphans and left them their estate."**

In our family, my father and paternal grandmother, Mary Eagy Carter, seem to have inherited the Springer lady's affinity for plants, for they were both noted for their skillful cultivation of beautiful flower beds.

My father, also named Charles, and his sister Abby, both remembered a visit from an uncle when they were very young. He arrived wearing an impressive bearskin coat and notified their mother that she was a Springer heir. The significance of this matter was further impressed upon her when in 1923 an attorney approached

---

* Elizabeth Montgomery, *Reminiscences of Wilmington*, Wilmington, Delaware: Johnston and Bogia, 1872.
**Ibid.

her on the same subject. At the time, a host of two thousand Springers was gathering in Chicago, all claiming direct descent from the eighteen kings and countless barons and medieval lords who were the forebears of Charles Christopher Springer, who had originally been granted by Lord Baltimore the two thousand acres of land on which the city of Wilmington is built. Springers sprang from everywhere, many of them sturdy sons of the soil, raisers of pumpkins and corn back in Iowa. These farmers, together with flappers and grandmothers, and Europeans and sleek-haired sheiks as well, all gathered and prepared for a legal battle involving an estate of five hundred million dollars' worth of Wilmington real estate, and a mausoleum in Stockholm, Sweden, purported to be the size of a house, each of its seven rooms filled with bushels of jewels and heirlooms.

This attorney urged my grandmother to join these other heirs in suing the owners of the DuPont powder mills, who ninety-nine years before had leased the land that had originally supported Charles Springer's farm. In 1923, that lease was up, and Springers' descendants had to prove their claims before the end of that year or forever relinquish their rights to the property.

To her credit, my grandmother was skeptical at the time and chose not to join the crowds of descendants flocking to Chicago, all claiming a share in this Arabian Nights fortune. And sure enough, later on the whole affair was exposed as a notorious scam.

Within the past thirty or forty years, however, a newspaper reported that a man named Springer in Chicago won a large sum of money from DuPont. Perhaps they paid it to avoid a nuisance suit. Persistence does have its small virtue.

73

A descendant of Ambassador Charles Springer: Great-Grandfather James Barlow Carter (1823–1896), Civil War veteran, Indiana Volunteer Infantry.

P.H. and the Runaway Pigs

ONE HOT JUNE DAY in the 1850s, my great-grandfather Patrick Henry Keegan, aged nineteen and just beginning his career as a railroad man, wiped his face with a big red kerchief while repeatedly looking over his shoulder at the livestock cars. Jim, the engineer, didn't prod him to keep the engine fired up, for he was just as curious and distracted as was "P.H."

The situation was unprecedented: the Michigan Southern Railroad was taking a chance in promising to haul three hundred porkers thirty-five miles from Monroe, Michigan to Toledo, Ohio in time to board the boat for Buffalo. Their daily run, starting at 5:30 A.M., usually covered sixty miles, from Monroe to Hillsdale, Michigan, but even traveling at a top speed of six miles per hour didn't give them much leeway. The road was rough and they had never hauled livestock before. P.H. just felt it in his bones — they were surely headed for trouble.

The pigs weighed about four hundred pounds each, all of them penned into flat cars with sides built up for the occasion. The drovers stood at each end and had quite a time of it, tapping the pigs with long poles, as the huge beasts pressed against the side-boards.

P.H. grinned at the sight of the drover, dressed in a fashionable frock coat with big brass buttons and wearing a high silk hat. His helper was a seven-foot tall, raw-boned, country boy.

Then P.H. held his breath as one pig rushed the side: the train's speed was increasing up to four or five miles an hour now, and the flatcars rocked back and forth on

Market Day in Castlepollard, County West Meath, Ireland, where P.H. Keegan lived until age seven. He then moved to a farm in what is now Harlem, New York City.

the jolting roadway, making the animals restless.

The third man in the cab anxiously watched the rails ahead, for sometimes, if the train were on a hill, it inexorably slowed down, and occasionally even came to a full stop. When that happened the workers carried buckets to the nearest farm to fetch sand, which was used to create traction so they could get the train moving again. Hopefully, today there would be no such untimely obstacles to prevent them from getting those pigs on the boat to Buffalo.

Imagining that scene, which took place nearly one hundred and fifty years ago, and contrasting it with the efficiency of train travel today, we marvel that the Michigan Southern moved at all. The old Baldwin engine didn't really have a cab, and there were only leather curtains to drop in case of rain. There was no bell, and the whistle was the size of a thimble. Towns just had to be on the watch, to see when and if the train were coming. It didn't need a headlight, for the train never ran at night. There was no danger of it blowing up, even without a steam gauge, as long as someone remembered to lean on the butcher's scale to hold the valve down. Sometimes, if Jim didn't feel like making the run, the train just stayed home that day. Clearly, train travel was rather casual in those days.

But today's run was an important one for the company, and P.H.'s heart beat a little faster watching the two drovers, who worked more and more frantically to herd the poor stumbling pigs away from the sides of the cars. P.H. thought the pigs seemed to be eyeing the big blackberry bushes along the line when. . . suddenly it happened.

77

Patrick Henry Keegan and family at home, Ft. Wayne, Indiana

First one, then several pigs began to leap off the cars. The drovers beat their poles and shouted, and Jim slowly pulled the engine to a halt. As if that were the signal, all three hundred pigs seemed to get the idea of freedom at once, and within minutes they were wildly running through the woods.

The tall country boy ran after them. His stride was impressive but the pigs were faster, and though the drover's coat-tails flew and his hat sailed off into the bushes, he was no more successful than the long-legged youth. The engineer began to laugh at the sight, and the crew members rolled helplessly on the ground in mirth.

The cause was lost. When the unhappy men finally gave up, half the pigs remained free, and the crew started up the engine once more, hoping at least to deliver the remaining hogs to Toledo by the deadline. They arrived too late, and the company lost a lot of money on the deal.

P.H.'s memorable journey with the first load of livestock conducted through Michigan Territory by rail gave him a story to tell over and over again for the rest of his days. In the telling of it he always sat back in his rocker and laughed as hard as he did when the mishap actually occurred. Great-Grandpa was a railroad man for fifty-three years, but he always said that that first livestock fiasco was the one ride that outshone all the rest.

Left: Great-grandfather, P.H. Keegan (1827 – 1914), Ft. Wayne, Indiana;
Right: Great Uncle, Charles Crall (1848 – 1923),

They Died Young

Two SETS OF LETTERS about the Civil War have been
preserved in the family. A letter from the first set is cau-
tionary, written by my great-grandfather, Charles Eagy to
his brother. He writes of the death of the youngest
brother, who had enlisted in the army and died from an
illness rather than in battle. The other set was written by
a young father to his wife, and describes both the bore-
dom and the sordid camp conditions he lived through
right up until he died.

The letter from Charles Eagy to his brother is dated "Indiana, 1863." It is full of homilies and spiritual advice
from a minister — which Charles was — speaking to a beloved brother whom he felt to be in need of guidance. The
younger brother John, who, like Charles, had been discharged from service, had died one week earlier from the
"Camp Darea" and a failed lung. The following is an excerpt from the letter:

"You was saying you was going to shoot a boy for hol-
lering for Jeff Davis. I say drop your powder horn for I
would not want to hear of you having to suffer by killing
anything that was so low lifed as to holler for Jeff
Davis, such people is beneath the notice of a sheep-
killing dog. Just pass them by and pay no attention to
them they will suffer more in the out-come than if they
was shot . . .

"The copperheads is cool as crackers here lately. They
find they are in a poor row for stumps so they keep cool.
You was saying everybody around you belonged to the union but yourself. I believe I would join too. I would not

wait to be left alone for fear they would take me for a copperhead too."

Copperheads were northern Peace Democrats, who favored compromise with the Confederacy and disagreed with Lincoln's intention to free slaves in the South. These copperheads remind us of southerners today who, when the Civil War is mentioned, still say, "You mean the war of aggression by the North." War never really ends. Bitter memories seem to last for generations.

Charles's letter continues:

"There has been a heavy battle fought by Rosencrans [Major General William S. Rosencrans — the Battle of Chicamauga] on the nineteenth and twentieth of last month. The sixty-eighth [his former regiment] was in it, but we have not heard yet who was hurt but expect when we do hear from them I will hear of some of my old bunkmates being killed and wounded. . . All that we have heard is that the regiment is cut to pieces. I hope old Rosy will be able to whip old Bragg and take the last one of them prisoners. I want this war to come to a close as soon as possible but not until the traitors is conquered if it takes ten years. I do not want it to stop until they are whipped."

General Braxton Bragg "won" the battle with a loss of seventy thousand men.

* * * * *

Tom Hawkins, eldest son of George and Abigail, wrote his wife Lydia regularly throughout the first part of 1865, after he left home as a volunteer in Company D of the 151st Indiana Regiment, until June when he was hospital-

82

Thomas W. Hawkins married Lydia McElwee in Vermont, and they had
one child Lela, a few weeks old when he heeded Lincoln's call for volun-
teers in the Civil War. He died in Andersonville of typhoid fever, twelve
days after writing Lydia that he'd be home soon. He never saw active
service, and his letters home speak of "filth and poor food." He was
twenty-three years older than my grandmother, Ida, but he's remembered
by us all.

ized. He was buried in Nashville, July 10th, 1865.

Thomas Hawkins was never in combat. His letters describe dreadful conditions in camp: crowding, poor food, much sickness, lack of necessities, and the utter futility of their being there at all. The cities of Petersburg and Richmond had already fallen, and though Lee surrendered on April 9 and the last Confederate troops lay down their arms by May 26, hundreds of Union men never went home again. In each letter Tom promises his wife that he'll be returning soon: in a few weeks; next week; by the 4th of July. . . and then came news that he had died from typhoid fever, far away from home in Tennessee.

His letters are literate and loving, and show the fine qualities of a would-be teacher, or perhaps a clergyman. Like so many others, he was a man whose destiny was cut short by the army's ineptitude, which may have been due in great part to lack of funds.

Tom's regiment never saw active service, but the men died by the hundreds anyway. Most of his short life had been spent in South Hero, Vermont, where he met and married Lydia and fathered his only daughter. Leah was three and a half weeks old when he left to participate in the Civil War. He died six months later of typhoid fever, at the age of twenty-nine. Though he died over a 150 years ago, Tom is not forgotten by his descendants. His daguerreotype shows the kind of person we'd like to know, and we wonder how much we lost because his life was cut so short. He wrote several times a week to Lydia, though her letters to him seldom arrived, and told her over and over how much he loved her, how he treasured the picture he carried of "our little pet." The letters are long, largely cheerful, and full of good advice. The following are excerpts, a few sentences taken from each letter.

"[No date] Richmond, it is said, is surely taken, and some thirty or forty thousand of the Rebels, a great many cannon with a large amount of other stores. So there will not be much more hard fighting, and you need not be uneasy about me getting wounded."

"[Peru, Indiana, February 2, 1865] This morning I leave for LaPorte. I had to walk all the way yesterday, and was almost tired out when I got in town.

I met Pop and Mother yesterday. When they were told that we [he and his cousin Thomas McElwee] had enlisted it seemed to surprise them a little."

"[Indianapolis, April 5] There are only about three thousand here [in camp]. I feel well, even better than I did yesterday. My stay in Camp Carrington will be short. I do not like the looks of it very well yet; so I am not sorry that I am going to leave soon.

The news about Richmond being taken is surely true. An immense number of prisoners and a great amount of stores are the trophies of victory."

[April 9] We found the company at this place in good spirits and most of them well. We are camped about a half mile west of a small town. It is a pretty place — good spring water to drink. The timbers all around for about a mile have been cut down. To the east is a fort. I passed several fortifications on the road here.

"Most of the country through which we passed showed the effects of war. I saw many houses or ruins. Large plantations were laid to the cannon, houses were burnt, and even those buildings left were mostly deserted. The people looked discouraged.

"Through part of Kentucky and as far as I came into Tennessee, there were plenty of peach trees. It is a great country for all kinds of fruit.

"Today it is raining very hard. Us boys are cooped up in our different tents, like so many chickens in a coop. The tents are quite comfortable, unless it rains very hard. For quite a long time they do not leak at all.

"I expect the regiment will stay here for some time. It has rained nearly every day, so there is no drilling or dress parade. There are quite a number of regiments camped in sight. Orders (not to go into Nashville) prevent any of the squad from deserting. One did get away; officers said if he was caught he would be handled very roughly."

"[Nashville, April 12] I arrived in Indianapolis Tuesday evening, next day went to the hospital for my things. They were not to be found. The ward master was not going to let me have anything, but I went to the commander, got an order from the chief clerk to the ward master. I did not get quite as much as was in mine; only one blanket, but fared better than some others that lost all.

"The next morning I and twenty others left for the regiment. We arrived at Jeffersonville on the Ohio River at night, then next day started for Louisville, Kentucky, and Nashville, Tennessee.

"We got our breakfast at Nashville at what is called the soldiers' home, then left for Tullahoma, where the regiment is situated. We slept that night in the captain's tent.

"The health of the regiment is good, a great deal better

than it was at Camp Carrington in Indianapolis. It is a healthy place where we are camped — good spring water to drink, and a nice creek running along beside the camp, for the boys to wash in.

"On the way from Indianapolis I got to see a good deal of the country. Some was very fine, while other portions were about as poor as I ever saw, quite destitute through Kentucky, and Tennessee as far as I have come. Most of the fences are gone and a great many houses are burnt."

"[Tullahoma, Tennessee, April 19] I would have got [letters from home] sooner if a railroad bridge between Nashville and here had not broken down. It took a week to repair. Last night six trains came through. An old settler told there was more cold rains here this spring than he ever knew. I was afraid it would make me sick again but it has not.

"In camp we take our tin of coffee, a piece of meat and bread; walk off to some place and sit down to eat or sit flat on the ground or stand up. We have drained rice, and corn and beans several times, so of course we live quite fair. Health in camp is tolerable, several complaining, unfit for guard or fatigue duty or to drill, yet not very sick.

"Lee and all his army was captured. Nathan Forrest, a Rebel general with his command in Alabama, was captured, also Mobile is taken, so there only remains Johnson and his army to take, the Rebels are completely used up. I do not think. . . the war will still last long.

"There were two hundred guns fired from this fort when we got the news of the capture of Lee and his army.

"Lydia, I wish you would send three or four papers to me to read. I have to pay ten cents for a paper here and it

87

is not worth such when I get it.

"It would make you laugh to see the boys in their little dog tents as they are called. You have to get down on your knees to get in them. Generally two persons, sometimes three, stay in the tent."

"[Nashville, possibly April 30] The regiments are very slow about getting organized. I suppose as soon as our regiment is organized we will all get furloughs for a few days. I have had good health since I came here.

"The barracks in which our company stay are good as can be expected. The 'bunk' or bed I sleep in is about as wide as a common bed. Three of us have to sleep in a bunk. Thomas McElwee and Henry Murdon are my bed fellows. We are somewhat crowded, yet we fair much better than some others. Some have to sleep on the floor, and as muddy as it is now, and has been for a week, was not very desirable.

"I have nothing to do, no duty of any kind. The reason is the regiment is not organized yet. Getting tired of laying still and doing nothing. Yesterday morning I went to the Suttles where they keep a boarding house, and got a chance to wash dishes all day. I made a dollar and best kind of boarding which was quite acceptable after having only bread, meat and poor coffee."

"[Tullahoma, May 18] Saturday there is to be a grand review of all the nine regiments encamped here. Some say the review is preparatory to being mustered out of the army.

"You spoke of joining the Regulars. There is no danger of me joining. I have left you once and gone to the Army;

when I get out of this you may be assured I will stay put, for there will never be any necessity of me going again. To tell the truth, I do not like a soldier's life at all.

"Staying here in camp when the immense number of men are not needed at all greatly increases desire to get home again. On every side and every day I hear [it].

"I would like to have been at the church to have gone to meeting with you. The old church must look quite well since it is fixed up."

"[Tullahoma, May 30] I am well and hearty as usual. The talk is that we will be sent home in a short time. But it takes time to do such a vast amount of business, to muster out, pay off, and discharge so many troops. Surely it will not be many weeks.

"Not far from the Fourth of July, this regiment and all of the one year men will be on their way home. I would really like to have been at home so as to have gone to the [church] raising, a church is needed very much there. I wrote home for postage stamps and more money; send it in your next letters."

"[Tullahoma, June 1] I was glad to hear the bees had swarmed and seemed to be doing well. But sorry to hear that Pa's bees went off. That money and stamps came, safe, only there was not enough of them. Three dollars will be all I need for a good while. I would not have been so near out but I lent over eight dollars.

"I am well, thanks be to heaven. I am stouter and heartier now than I have been for the past two years. But there are several sick, two of this company in the hospital in town, six have died.

"Without a doubt, as soon as it can be done, all the soldiers except the regulars will be discharged, for it was never known in all the annals of history where such a large army was kept by, after a war was well over."

"[Tullahoma, June 5] I have borrowed stamps of Thomas McElwee until you send me some. Postage stamps can not be got at this place. I have tried to buy them several times. I have about a dollar in money yet, so send me some money. I have lived as saving as possible and was in hopes I would not need any more than I brought from home. But I have had to buy some things to eat many times, or go half starved. There is also many other little notions pertaining to camp to buy — blacking for boots, nails to fix our shanty at twenty cents a pound.

"I am well and hearty. I still think I will be in old Indiana the Fourth of July, next, such is the general impression in camp. You said the old hog had such a nice litter of pigs. Try and feed her plenty of slops so she will do well always. I was glad to hear about the flax, that it was so good; you spoke of having it wove for socks. It would be a good plan."

"[Knoxville, June 20]" I slept with the rest of the boys on this post on the porch of the house we are stationed at. I slept very comfortable.

"I have heard but one sermon since I came to the regiment, and that was very short and poorly delivered.

"You want the price of our place. Fifteen hundred dollars is the price. If the railroad goes through, as it surely will in time, there is but little inducement to sell it at present unless the money could immediately be made use of to a good advantage or another place bought right off. Do what you think is best.

"Send me five dollars. I will have to buy a few vegetables, occasionally, as well as some medicine. It is a sickly [place] us boys are in, and the sour bread and the sour belly (as pork is called) and often fresh beef as tough as leather almost. Such food and the unhealthy place is bringing boys down sick by the dozens. I am not very well myself, but am still able to fill my place in the ranks.

"Business is reviving quite fast in Nashville. There are several large buildings being erected and others that had been commenced are being finished, yet the effects of the war are evident and can be seen on every side.

"I have seen upwards of a thousand prisoners since I came to Nashville. All of them seem very glad to return to their home again. Some seemed quite ready to answer all questions, while others were quite sullen and seemed little inclined to talk. They were all dressed with various kinds of clothes, mostly gray or butternut color, some appeared genteel while others looked shabby and squalid.

"You said there had been a box of things sent to me. I was over to the depot to see if it had arrived yet but it had not come this morning. I will be very glad to get the box for this grub us boys eat in camp is none the less palatable; a little better than at Tullahoma, but a person gets very tired of the same 'victuals' every day without any knickknacks at all for a change occasionally.

"If I had plenty of money knickknacks of all kinds could be purchased in town. At Tullahoma everything was so very high, and not fit to eat, hardly, when a person had purchased them. Here in Nashville vegetables have been raised and an abundance of various articles sold."

91

Tom's last letter was dated June 28, four days after the letter quoted above was written. He wrote that he was very sick, staying in the hospital, and made reference to the filth and poor food. He died and was buried in Nashville only twelve days after the last letter quoted. His body was sent to Indiana for reburial, on February 27, 1866. There were charges of twenty-five dollars for shipping "one corpse" from Indianapolis to Peru, and forty dollars for "one zinc case."

Tom is still a personage to us all.

Sure Cures

ASAFETIDA IS INCLUDED IN the list of medicines taken by Sir John Hawkins on his final voyage to America in 1595. Superstitions die hard. Centuries later, as a child I was sent to school with a stinking sack of asafetida around my neck, to hold off something or other. It held off people, that's for sure, so in a backhanded way I suppose it did hold off germs.

My grandmother, Mary Eagy Carter (1853–1920) of South Bend, Indiana, concocted a miracle salve that became famous in our family and among her friends. The salve not only healed burns, but also closed cuts overnight, and drew thorns and cockleburs out of the skin. Grandma Carter even sold it to the Studebaker wagon factory to cure cuts on their horses.

Mary had once nursed a German neighbor through an illness, and as a mark of her gratitude, the latter had passed on the salve recipe to my grandmother. The recipe is as follows.

Mary boiled one part each of beeswax, mutton tallow, and resin, and two parts of linseed oil. Fully blended, the mixture was easy to apply when strained and cooled. Elderberry bark was another ingredient, helpful though not essential, and was added to the blend whenever the boys could find it along the Indiana river banks. Nowadays the ingredients are a bit harder to find. Beeswax is found in hardware stores, where it is sold to plumbers for setting toilet seats. The butcher has mutton tallow (if he's a young man, ask for hard fat of sheep), and resin can be found in a music store. Linseed oil can be bought in a

paint store, though the old-fashioned kind, which is oilier, is better because it doesn't cake when cool.

In addition to the salve, medications seventy-five years ago included Carter's Little Liver Pills, Vick's Vapo Rub, caster oil, Mentholatum, hog or bacon fat for an infected cut (if we were out of Grandma's salve), mustard plaster on the chest for a cough, and Smith Brothers Cough Drops if we didn't happen to have any horehound in the house. What we couldn't cure at home we took to Dr. Craig in Shawnee, Oklahoma, an elderly "rubbing doctor" with a tobacco-stained white beard. He cured Grandma Ida Keegan's rheumatism, and also my foot, which turned gangrenous after I cut it walking barefoot in the chicken pen collecting eggs. In addition to rubbing, he advocated drinking large amounts of artesian well water, kept in big glass jugs which he had rubbed with his dry, warm hands. We kept the jugs in a swinging wire frame hung in the kitchen, supported by a metal standard on the floor.

I suppose today we'd call him a magnetic healer.

For head colds we sniffed salt water — a hateful treatment, but it worked. Sometimes, instead of sniffing the salt water, we bent over a steaming kettle with a towel thrown over the head.

Bengay, which later was used on the chest, was a little easier to take than the mustard plaster.

A Chrismas Greeting from Gramma to her three little girls,
For goodness and sweetness, they are jewels, real pearls.
This morning, Mother Earth is dressed up all in white;
Jack Frost gave her a gift last night,
A dress of white lace, so dainty and fine,
To make her look lovely at Christmas time.
Over wires, bushes and tree tops tall,
Down to the tiniest grass blade, he let this lace fall.
He sprinkled it over with diamonds so bright,
That sparkle and flash in the warm sunlight.
It's just like fairyland, so it seems to me;
Wish you girlies were here, it's beauty to see.
I suppose Santa Clause a visit will pay,
To you three little girls on Christmas Day,
Will leave you all some nice little toys,
That will make the New Year full of gladness and joys.

We send our love, and wish you all three,
A happy Christmas as ever could be.
May each day of the coming New Year
Be full of health, happiness, and all good cheer.

Grandmother and Grandfather Carter

Good Old
Golden Rule Days

URING THE CIVIL WAR, when male school teachers largely disappeared into military service, one might expect that the women who replaced them would have lent a softer touch in disciplining their students. However, my grandfather Harry Keegan was a young handful, and his parents finally resorted to sending him to a parochial school, where the policy was never to spare the rod. In my grandfather's words:

"When Father told me to stack the firewood, he caught me throwing it over the back fence instead. He took me by the collar and marched me down the street to a strict Catholic school. I wasn't much easier to handle there either. For a long time I thought teachers wore those long robes to hide the strap all of them seemed to keep hidden there."

My grandmother Ida, on the other hand, whom Harry would one day woo and wed, was a flower of docile obedience and girlish charm. Perhaps this was due in part to the fact that she was the youngest child of George and Jane Hawkins' rather large brood, and therefore received a lot of coddling. Too, with her peaches and cream complexion and sweet disposition, she was a very popular and pretty young lady and attracted many beaux.

Ida went on to graduate as valedictorian of her high school class, in Fort Wayne, Indiana. The year was 1876, and her sister Vic designed her dress for the occasion. My great aunt Vic has since described to me this labor of love, and we cannot doubt that Ida's gown was the es-

96

Ida Marie Hakins, age 18, 1876, valedictorian of her graduation class at Ft. Wayne High School; her dress was of lavender-gray taffeta, covered with knife pleatings of net, her nose-gay was given to her by Gene Stratton, later to become Gene Stratton Porter, the novelist and naturalist.

sence of chic for those times: a pastel lavender gray taffeta, covered with knife pleats of white net, grandly enhanced with a ruffled train. She carried a nosegay, specially gathered for her by her close friend, Gene Stratton Porter, who later became the well-known naturalist and novelist. Throughout the day the ushers added more flowers, as spontaneous tribute to Grandma's lovely presentation. Ida went on to accept a teaching position in a rural school, where one beau used to follow her for algebra lessons.

My mother, Cosette Keegan, graduated with the first class of trained kindergarten teachers at Friend's University in Wichita, Kansas. Following in her mother's footsteps, she also taught school, in Fort Wayne, Indiana and later in Oklahoma, where she became the first kindergarten teacher in the Territory.

When I asked her what she remembered about her first teaching experiences, she recollected seeing one of her five-year-old pupils in Fort Wayne carrying a bucket of beer to her father at work. And what about her memories of Chandler, Oklahoma, where there hadn't ever been the possibility for children to attend kindergarten before she came along?

"I had a terrible time working up a class," said my mother. "I went around door to door, inviting the parents to cookies and tea, when I would explain what their children would learn. But they were slow to send them. One mother said, 'I ain't going to send *my* kid to school to get licked!'

"My first and only pupil for a while was Cousin Roy and Estelle Hoffman's daughter, Dorothy. My most vivid memory of that first year is the time I lost the key to the

Grandma Ida Hawkins Keegan and her baby, Ercell, taken about 1889.

front door of the Court House, where I was given a room to hold my class. The City Fathers were put out with me, to say the least. My handsome older brother Ed was the very young mayor then.

"It was easier after I moved to Shawnee, where my family lived. The First North Methodist Episcopal Church, on the east side of town, let me set up a room in the basement with my excellent Froebel teaching materials, and I soon had all the boys and girls I could handle."

My two sisters and I in later years were also brought up on those really exciting materials, and all of us learned to read at an early age. Continuing in the family tradition, we three women went on to teach: Alice and Gene taught cello and violin, respectively, and I taught nursery school and volunteered as a literacy tutor for both adults and children. My daughter, Gene Nora, studied aviation and taught as a flight instructor for some years. Most of her students were men, but she remembers one image of those early days, of a determined girl in parachute straps, walking across the air field in a bouffant skirt, the wind blowing it out in all directions.

During World War II, Mother was asked to fill in for the teachers who had gone overseas. People claimed that without her there never would have been a kindergarten at the Shidler School in Oklahoma City, which was just south of the North Canadian River in a poor section of town. Her teaching license had long since expired, but her dedication to the students certainly had not, and in recognition of this far more important consideration the school board ignored both her unofficial status and her unorthodox teaching methods.

Mother broke all the rules: she threw notices of teach-

The graduating class in Fort Wayne, Indiana with Great-Aunt Abigail Keegan (1864–1958) to the extreme right. There were a few boys in the class, but either they were not important enough, or their clothes were not as pretty.

ers' meetings in the waste basket, and didn't bother to attend; she opened class with a prayer and spanked children when necessary. Both customs were illegal, but nobody cared and she was adored by all, students and parents alike. A hugely nurturing presence in many peoples' lives, she didn't hesitate to take children home to wash their heads. She begged clothes for them from friends. My mother had a lot of heart.

Westerners Forward

I WAS BORN IN 1910, three years after Oklahoma Territory achieved statehood, and only twenty years after the last wild buffalo was killed in the Panhandle. I watched cowpaths made over into great stretches of paved highway. The first one crossing the entire state was completed in 1930. The state capitol was built in Oklahoma City. I attended the inaugural barbecue and ball of a newly elected governor and subsequently had a small part in his impeachment proceedings.

I saw the land that was once stark prairie grass suddenly transformed into the richest low gravity oil fields in the world, and I knew the first names of the farmers who got rich overnight from it. I helped in the first struggles of Oklahoma's tentative reaching out to the fine arts . . . and went to sleep in the hot peanut gallery on opening night of the first grand opera performance in Oklahoma City.

The state was arguably the most discouraging one in the country for performers in the fine arts. Paderewski, normally so generous with encores, was called back only once at his debut in our state.

It was a fight to live in Oklahoma but we had the strengthening joy of battling against the odds.

The beauty of trees is one of the dearest things in the world to me. Today I lie awake in Boise, Idaho, watching shapes of swaying branches against the night sky, sometimes pricked with the light of stars, the moon, or distant passing jets.

But only blackjack, scrub oak, and cottonwoods were native to the red soil of the part of Oklahoma where I

lived. They were never tall and stately. My favorite Oklahoma tree was the pecan, for we could go out along
almost any creek, and with blankets and sticks knock
down all the nuts we could eat.

Winds blew continuously. Cyclones swooped down
and caused great damage, once taking away the top floor
in the school where I had studied. Red dirt and sand
sifted through crevices in a way that was impossible to
prevent. Sometimes an oil well ran wild, covering anyone
even miles away with a thin coating of black grease,
which had to be scraped and sandpapered off. In winter
the river dried up and there were few lakes.

Does it sound like the last place in the world to choose
to live? Don't you believe it. Oklahoma was young country, vital and exciting. For two years, even after the Great
Depression of 1929 had begun, Oklahoma City was the
center of business activity for the entire region. More buy-
ing and selling was done there than ever before, and
building construction per person was the greatest in the
entire Southwest. Main Street traffic resembled Chicago's
Michigan Boulevard at 5:15 P.M. The state produced Pat
Hurley, Secretary of War, and Will Rogers, the happiest
and most widely loved entertainer in the country.

We Oklahomans have always been activity personified.
Sometimes we move too fast, managing our affairs awk-
wardly, like a baby learning to walk: falling down again
and again, and again and again getting back on our feet
and moving on. When in later years our banks failed due
to an exaggerated optimism and a too generous handling
of loans, we even did that on a grand scale, by taking
down giant banks in other states with us.

Perhaps we're more like a growing puppy, stumbling

over our own feet in our hurry to get there. But what animal can you think of that is happier than a puppy? We may not be pedigreed, but we catch more rabbits, and I suspect we get more fun out of daily existence than the handsome, well-groomed dogs preening in show rooms.

We are, and were, and always will be pioneers. We're westerners, Oklahomans, and proud of it.

The Run for Land

RIFLE SHOTS AT midday on April 22, 1889 initiated the official opening of the greatest land rush in American history.

The government had bought two million acres of land in central Oklahoma from the Creek and Seminole Indian tribes, with the intention that this free land be possessed and settled by the first people who came to stake their claims on it, on this dramatically historic day.

In addition to the early comers, fifteen thousand people arrived on the first day, and two towns, Guthrie and Oklahoma Station, became cities of ten thousand people overnight. People came by train, on horseback, in buggies and wagons, and on foot. They came from Canada and Europe as well, with ten thousand arriving from Liverpool alone one week before the run. Thousands sneaked over the line guarded by armed soldiers. They hoped to stake out early claims and get a good location, for to be a land-owner was highly desirable, yet often impossible, particularly in Europe and Canada.

One day before the opening of the lands, Roy Hoffman, twenty-year-old grandson of George Hawkins, rode into Guthrie on the Santa Fe Railroad, traveling from the border of the Unassigned Lands. A reporter with the *St. Louis Globe Republic*, he arrived with a blanket and a gunny-sack filled with five dollars' worth of canned goods. He set up a typewriter on the corner of a table in the land office, housed in the only building in Guthrie at the time, and the next day wired his first story about the day of the "Run." Technically, he was a "Sooner," but he was there

Ten seconds after the gun, the race into the Cherokee Outlet, September 16, 1893. Photo credit claimed by both P.A. Miller and Thomas Croft, employed that day by W. S. Prettyman, Arkansas City, Kansas. Courtesy of Archives and Manuscripts Division of the Oklahoma Historical Society.

on newspaper business. Today, any native Oklahoman is called a Sooner, but back then, anyone who jumped the opening gun deserved the title.

The new and hastily put together towns were harum-scarum spectacles of white tents, log cabins, shacks, and cattle pens. In Oklahoma City the post office started out in an old chicken house, and just three years later that town boasted a three-story brick building at the crossing of Main Street and Broadway: it looked like and already was a city.

Roy's stories described the total lack of amenities that existed when he arrived. There was no housing, no kerosene or wood for heating, no stores for supplies and food, no toilet facilities, and no drinking water. Housewives hadn't the means for cleaning lamp chimneys, nor were there stoves where irons could be heated for pressing the family's clothes. They had been accustomed to pumping water from wells, and carrying out slop jars to outhouses. These homely conveniences did not exist for the ambitious land runners, who were thrown back to a primitive level of survival where even the most basic resources could not be taken for granted.

Roy wrote that drinking water, muddy river water dispensed from buckets, cost ten cents a glass. Though a dining room housed in a tent was able to accommodate only a small portion of the crowd, fifty-cent meals brought in a profit of fifteen hundred dollars the first day. Most people brought or fashioned shelter of some kind, including covered wagons, shacks, and "soddies" built of sod squares or bricks. Many shelters were dug partly underground, and there were tents as far as the eye could see, all along the borders of the Unassigned Lands. One man had his home dragged in on rollers.

Naturally, everyone sought the choicest sections of land on which to make a claim, either in the town, or in rural lots. In Guthrie, some people staked out locations in areas that had already been designated as the city's streets. Thousands had camped out for as long as a year, right along the boundaries where soldiers had been posted with Winchesters and double-barreled shotguns, holding back the would-be Sooners from entering ahead of the designated time. These people were often disappointed and turned back later on, finding all the most desirable sites already taken by "illegals," that is, by Sooners who had persisted and dared literally to jump the gun, staking their claims before the opening rifle shots were sounded.

Located southeast of the Sauk and Fox Agency was a town of Sooners called Shawneetown, an Indian village on the Red Plains where some of my family were born. The Agency itself was a parcel of land that had been designated by the government for the Sauk and Fox Indians, one of the land's functions being to provide a headquarters where Indians could come by to pick up their quarterly payments on what was called Allotment Day. These payments were issued by the government as compensation for having appropriated the land from the Indians, though the method of dispensing these allotments was one that was sometimes subject to corruption.

While the primary inhabitants on the agency were Indians, those holding positions of authority and power — such as the shopkeepers and teachers — were all white people. The paymaster, that is, the one who dispensed the quarterly allotments, was a white person as well. Roy's father, my Great Uncle Pete Hoffman, ran the store with his partner Charles Conklin; the latter's daughter, Estelle, eventually married Roy. Roy's first job at the Agency was working as a horse wrangler on the Whistler Ranch. Later on the job of handing out the quarterly allotments to the Indians passed on to Roy from the Sauk and Fox agent's son, Lee Patrick. Lee later married my cousin, Cosette Stratton.

While Indians believed in cooperation in the use of commonly shared land, pioneers brought with them the European notion of land ownership and competition in acquiring private property. "Private property" was a concept unknown to the Indian way of life, which was classless, free, easy, and unconstrained. Many white captives, having tasted it, chose not to return to the white man's civilization when they were once again given the chance to do so. On the other hand, there were many pioneers who could not understand the Indian's lack of interest in hard work. The Indians, for their part, could never understand the white man's greed and habit of acquisition. Indians were never successfully enslaved, nor were they ever made into a working class.

Roy's wife Estelle wrote what it was like to live on the Agency: "It was a land of no section lines, no fences, timber and prairies all in an absolute state of nature, untouched by man." The Indian encampment behind the Agency on the eve of their quarterly payments, or on holidays, was "like a bee hive," Estelle wrote. "Teepees appeared, painted, with a hole at the top to let out the smoke, or in warm weather, circular, netting covered shelters were raised; open fires, with a kettle swung over them, meat suspended over the fire, or sometimes a dog roasting.

"We thought it great fun to go down and walk among the camps, see the lazy bucks, the busy squaws in their finery, hundreds of dogs, the babies strapped and wrapped on a board which the squaw could easily carry on her back or leave hanging or leaning on a tree while she was busy.

"The squaws wore full skirts of brilliant calico. If the predominant color was red, some way would be found to introduce piping or trimming of green, purple or another color. The shirt worn with tail outside was often of black sateen. . . The navy blue broadcloth used for the men's breech clout, leggings, sometimes for the wampum-trimmed vest, was of the finest, heaviest, softest quality. It was called 'fancy list.'

"The blanket Indians, bareheaded, wore the head shaved except for a roach from the forehead in a narrow strip to the back. This was called 'mochon.' Women wore theirs greased and slicked back, wound with tape into a thick club about nine inches long. Roy and Lee Patrick, son of the agent, both shaved their heads one time, Indian fashion, and from that time on the Indians called them 'Mochon.' Father always said that the Indians were very honorable and trustworthy. . . .

"Hunting in the early day was of course marvelous. Deer and turkey were plentiful, and an occasional wild boar with huge tusks, and quail by the million."*

*   *   *   *   *

* Estelle Hoffman, *I Remember for My Children*, Oklahoma City, privately published, 1948.

My mother, Cosette Keegan, was filled with the spirited enthusiasm of those days. Together with a girl friend she made a run herself on horseback. They were too young to file for actual ownership of the land, but nonetheless they did stake out their acreage, and then gave it to the first man who came along and wanted it.

Harriet's story is more typical. In 1891, when she was twenty-one years old and therefore eligible to do so, she and her brother Lee Patrick chose their hundred and sixty acres apiece of government land on the Creek County line, and made their run for it. Harriet rode sidesaddle on a beautiful horse her father had given her, wearing a blue calico dress with a velvet yoke, collar, and cuffs. Her best riding habit was too long to be safe: the sweeping skirts were not suited to a swift run. Cosette Stratton, my Great Aunt Vic's daughter, later on to be married to Lee Patrick, joined them, riding on the front seat of a wagon and holding a lantern in her lap. Lee's claim adjoined Harriet's to the north, and Cosette drove her stakes immediately west of Lee's.

Harriet, with her brother's help, built a one-room frame house on her allotment, fenced in her acreage with barbed wire, and eagerly planted nine dollars' worth of potatoes. She and Lee witched for water and dug a fine well.

In fact, they ate only one meal from their potato crop before it failed. They bought cattle, but the entire herd died of measles. Their hogs, safely penned in a hog-tight fence, were ravaged by cholera, and as a final mishap, the flood gates they had built on the creek washed away.

In 1894, like many other pioneers who sank under just one calamity too many, Harriet gave up, and a lawyer from Oklahoma City bought her land claim for three thousand dollars.

Yet, there was some kind of inner strength in these pioneers, a stamina that renourished itself under adversity, and the examples of my peoples' lives illustrates that fact: the land-running men went on to pursue careers in banking in Stroud and several other cities throughout Oklahoma, and Harriet pursued her profession as a teacher, eventually claiming Jim Thorpe as one of her pupils.

* * * * *

In 1896, after "proving up" her one hundred and sixty acres for the prescribed five years, Harriet moved on to the next phase of her life and began teaching at Haskell Institute, an Indian school in Kansas. In her class there were twin eight-year-old boys, named Jim and Charles Thorpe. During a measles epidemic Charles caught pneumonia and died in her arms. Jim continued on as her student.

When he was a student at the Indian Industrial School in Carlisle, Pennsylvania, Jim Thorpe was called "the greatest football player of all time." King Gustav V of Sweden referred to him as "The greatest athlete in the world." During the 1912 Olympic games he was the first athlete ever to win both the Decathlon and the Pentathlon, and in 1951 he was one of the first men to be honored with membership in the National Football Foundaton's Hall of Fame.

In 1970, on her one hundredth birthday, two years before she died, Harriet was interviewed by a *Daily*

Oklahoman newspaper reporter. She was asked what she remembered about Jim Thorpe in the classroom.

"Oh, I'll never forget him," she said. "He was the best student I ever had at flipping flies with a rubber band. There were no screens on the windows then, you know."

Evidently he had athletic ability even then.

Chandler, Oklahoma

NOT ONLY WERE family members active in the early days of Guthrie, Oklahoma City, and the Sauk and Fox Agency, they also played a part in the early history of Chandler, in Oklahoma Territory.

In 1891, Great Uncle Pete Hoffman, left his position as manager of the store in the Sauk and Fox Agency and struck out for Chandler. He rode into the new town with a wagon full of merchandise. Agent Lee Patrick had told him which would be the most desirable place in town to set up business, and on that prominent corner he set up a general store in a tent. Grandpa Harry H. Keegan accompanied him.

No one ever told me what Grandpa was doing there. But his older sister, Abigail Choate Keegan, once wrote me that he had a wandering foot, and "always knew the grass was greener on the other side of the street." He probably didn't want to get left out of all the excitement. Mother told me that he left Grandma and the children to go traveling, leaving them behind to sell produce to the neighbors on their farm in Wichita, Kansas. He was a railroad man and had passes. He made a trip to the World's Fair in Philadelphia in 1876, and once he went to Mexico, where he bought an opal ring for Abbie, which she later willed to me.

At any rate, Grandpa did make at least one run for land with Pete, went back home, and soon moved the whole family to Shawnee. While living there, Mother taught kindergarten in Chandler, and her older brother, Ed Keegan, became the young mayor of the same bustling

Otis Claire Keegan   *Edwin Keegan*

Grandma's family, the Keegans: Back row: Ocie, Ed's wife; Art; Ercell; Claire, Ed's son; Front row, Homer; Harry; Tom, Ed's son; Ida; Cosette; Ed. 1907.

Harry Keegan   *Patrick Henry Keegan*

South Manvel Ave., Chandler, OK, summer 1895. Courtesy of Archives and Manuscripts Division of the Oklahoma Historical Society.

town. Later on he served in the legislature, and after Pete's corner store became the Union National Bank, Ed began a long career in banking there. He married, built a fine home, and bore two sons. The elder, Claire, captained his football team, went off to West Point, graduated from Oklahoma State University, and eventually became successful in the oil business in Tulsa. He married his childhood sweetheart, Mary Collar. They had three children. The younger son, Tom, who all his life would have preferred farming, succeeded his father in the bank, married, and raised his two children in Chandler.

Pete's son Roy and his wife Estelle had a lovely home in Chandler, and their daughter Dorothy was Mother's first kindergarten pupil. The house, which was filled with family mementos, burned down one night while they were away attending a dance, and all keepsakes were lost.

It was at Roy's home that the only family story of buried treasure originated. One day their hired man uncovered a big sack of ancient coins while digging under an old tree. It was decided that some bank robber had buried it there because it was too heavy to carry and never did come back for it. No one ever claimed the treasure.

Grandfather, Harry Howard Keegan, born in Adrian Michigan, 1854.

Brothers Claire and Tom Keegan

When Henry Starr
Robbed Lee's Bank

COUSIN COSETTE Stratton Patrick (1871–1966) received many offers to buy Henry Starr's rifle, but she held on to it for years before donating it through her son to a museum in Chandler, Oklahoma. On March 27, 1915, Starr, one of the famed Western bandits of the early days in Oklahoma, used this rifle to hold up the National Bank in Stroud, Oklahoma, while other members of his gang were simultaneously robbing another bank down the street. Stroud made off with about two thousand dollars, while his pals netted twice that.

Lee Patrick (1868–1929), Cosette's husband and vice-president of the National Bank, was more upset at losing his mother's diamond than he was over the general theft. Under gunpoint, he was forced to remove the bank's funds from a cannon ball safe, hand them over to Starr, and then set the time lock. Using Lee Patrick as a shield, Starr escaped out the back door, only to be shot down from another alley behind the other bank where his cohorts were wrapping up their own business. Lee escaped unhurt, and Starr was sent to a doctor.

Lee's daughter, Alice, aged fourteen, witnessing the outbreak of this doomed escapade, raced home on her bike, screaming, "They are robbing the bank and killing papa!"

Cosette rushed to the bank. On discovering that her husband was all right but that his mother's diamond was gone, she sent him upstairs to the doctor's office to try to get it back from Starr. Lee and Starr knew each other, and Starr not only gave up the diamond, which had fallen

ooking east down 3rd Street, Stroud, Oklahoma Territory, during cotton market, October
3, 1906. Photo by H.C. Chaufty, Stroud. Courtesy of Archives and Manuscripts Division
f the Oklahoma Historical Society.

Henry Starr, a Cherokee and bank robber. Courtesy of Archives and Manuscripts Division of the Oklahoma Historical Society.

through a hole in the lining of his pocket, but he also gave up his rifle to Lee. Starr, expecting to make a big haul, had been a bit disgusted by the turn of events, and perhaps a little embarrassed as well:

"Hell," he told Lee. "If I'd known that was all there was, we wouldn't have staged the robbery."

Later, with several years of prison under his belt, Starr was invited back to Stroud, this time to act as a consultant for a film about the double robbery that he had bungled there some years before.

Six years later he was killed in another attempted robbery in Harrison, Arkansas.

The Marshal Who
Didn't Believe in Shooting

BILL TILGHMAN (1859–1924) — marksman, buffalo
hunter, Army scout, and Indian trader — was famed primarily as one of the greatest peace officers of the frontier
West. Serving as a lawman for forty-six years in Kansas
and Oklahoma, he never shot at another human being if
there were any way to avoid it.

My people claim him as a "shirttail relative"; that is,
there is strong evidence of kinship through his marriage
to Zoe Stratton, but so far we have been content merely to
assume our connection, without doing any conclusive re-
search to confirm it.

Tilghman began his career of "protecting" others at the
age of eight, in Fort Dodge, Iowa, when his father went off
to the Civil War and young Bill was already needed by his
family. He grew to be a gentle man who never smoked,
drank, or used foul language. He was recognized as being
a man of honor and consideration, traits that endeared
him to the Indians whom he befriended.

Despite his peaceful nature, Tilghman was known to
be an expert marksman, with both rifle and pistol, and
once rode two thousand miles in a successful trail after a
bandit. According to legend he shot three thousand buffaloes in seven months, thus achieving an all-time record,
while supplying meat to railroaders in the 1870s.

Bill was so shy and slow when courting his first wife
Flora that in the meantime she married someone else.
However, she was soon widowed and one year later they
were wed. Though Tilghman loved being a lawman, to

124

Flora's delight he became a successful rancher for a time on land that he homesteaded near Chandler, Oklahoma. In 1899 he started the first thoroughbred stock farm in the Territory, with two Kentucky stallions, and it was a great success. Nonetheless, when he was elected Lincoln county sheriff he couldn't resist a call back to the work he did best: taming outlaws and gunfighters.

His second wife, Zoe Stratton, was a pretty young woman who was twenty-six years his junior. The daughter of Mayo Stratton, fellow rancher and horseman, Zoe was independent and well-educated, and she herself rode, roped, and branded cattle as well as any cowboy. It is through Zoe that the Strattons in my family have assumed their kinship with Tilghman. True or not, his qualities of unflinching precision and dedication to accomplishing what needed to be done, tempered with compassionate restraint, make the example of his life stories interesting and inspiring for anyone's ears.

During his term as deputy sheriff, Tilghman was asked to bring in Bill Doolin, a notorious and dangerous outlaw. It was considered an impossibility. Refusing a posse of twenty men, Tilghman trailed the elusive badman for months, until the two men finally met each other in a bathhouse. The details of this unexpected encounter are unknown, but the results were that Tilghman succeeded in bringing in Doolin single-handedly, and most remarkably, without gunfire.

In later years Tilghman's quarry included bank robbers, horse rustlers, and cattle thieves. In those days of the "Wild West," Dodge City was teeming with cowboys trailing Texas longhorns, and it was there that Tilghman served as deputy for several years under Bat Masterson. When the oil boom reached its peak in Seminole, Okla-

125

homa, Bill became a bouncer there at Ma Murphy's dance hall. Finally, as Chief of Police in Oklahoma City, he became known as the man who drove outlaws out of Oklahoma. The Dalton gang were among the desperadoes he went after.

In 1915 Bill's career took another turn. In recognition of his expertise in dealing with outlaws, this versatile man supervised production of, and acted in, a western movie.

Beyond the sphere of keeping law and order as a gunman, Tilghman also supervised the first Oklahoma State Fair, and from there went on to become a state senator. President Theodore Roosevelt often welcomed him as a friend in the White House.

Five years later in 1924, while serving as police chief in the brawling oil town of Cromwell, Oklahoma, Bill heeded a call for help and was shot by a drunken roisterer. Thus was Bill Tilghman's life ended, at the age of seventy-one, while he was still trying to keep the peace.

None could better this legendary giant of a man in the use of firearms, but he shunned the use of them, often endangering his own life. That he would finally be felled in a common brawl was sadly ironic. He lay in state in the Capital building, and many notables subsequently attended his burial. Among his pallbearers were Governor Martin E. Trapp, ex-Governor J. B. Robertson, and Brigadier General Roy Hoffman. As Teddy Roosevelt said of him, he was a "Bully" man, a man his family and the state and nation could be proud of.

The Great Big Barbecue

IN JANUARY OF 1923, governor-elect Jack Walton invited everyone in Oklahoma to come to his inaugural ball and barbecue. Two hundred thousand people arrived from eighteen states, and it took a mini-army of three thousand pit men, waiters, and guards to serve us. I was twelve years old at the time and still remember waiting in line for my parents at the iron coffee urns that were as big as houses and served up twenty thousand gallons of coffee. I remember too how the tin cups of coffee burned our hands.

Thousands of people had jumped the gun at the fairgrounds, and sixty thousand more were served by evening, at the rate of fifteen persons per minute. Great charcoal pits had roasted five hundred head of beef the night before, and the crowds consumed prodigious amounts the following day: five hundred chickens, two hundred hogs, two hundred opossums, two hundred sheep, three thousand rabbits, one thousand squirrels, one thousand turkeys, and countless buffaloes, antelopes, bears, deer, ducks, frogs, and geese. I ate one barbecue sandwich.

Along with the meat, there were mountains of sweet potatoes, one hundred thousand loaves of bread, and an equal number of buns, with two hundred and fifty bushels of onions. There were thousands of sliced pickles.

Folk started arriving many days in advance. Whole Indian tribes showed up in beautifully colored blankets, some in feathered headdresses. Camped out at the fairgrounds west of the barbecue pits were the Cheyenne,

127

Arapahoe, Osage, Creek, Cherokee, and others as well. Hundreds of workers scurried among the different tribes. The weather was lovely — dry and warm for mid-winter.

Men built up fires in the pits, tended critters turning on the spits, and got up steam in the fire engines which kept the coffee urns perking. Guards roped off working areas, but the Indians were hungry and crowded in wherever food was ready.

As for the inaugural parade, every early-day Oklahoman was represented. There were pioneers in calico and bib overalls, fiddlers and clowns. There were conestogas, cowboys, and stage coaches: oil field teamsters driving six oxen yokes. Cousin Jim Carter played with one of the college bands, and a single plane flew overhead.

At the statehouse we shook hands with the governor and squeezed through enormous crowds. There were ladies in evening dress, and cowboys in spurs and chaps. Moccasined Indians pressed elbow to elbow on the marble stairs, and twenty-five bands played for those who cared to dance. Governor Walton led the grand march of all who had gathered: cowboys with guns in holster, Mexicans, Guardsmen, oil magnates, pensioners, and old soldiers. All wanted to welcome this popular new leader.

The parade and ball were more colorful, I suppose, but it was the "biggest barbecue in the world" that made the most lasting impression on me. Jack Walton kept all the promises he had made to the people of Oklahoma, as far as he could, but many of those promises were based on hot air. Nine months later he was removed from office.

The Impeachment of
Governor Jack Walton

IN OCTOBER, 1923, the Oklahoma legislature met to impeach Governor Jack Walton. My father, Charles E. Carter, was serving as secretary to Lieutenant Governor M. E. Trapp at the time and was also appointed to head the corps of court reporters at the trial. This was not an easy job: while legislators shouted at one another and behaved in an unseemly fashion, Daddy was obliged to take down every word, as well as dodge the ink wells that the "statesmen" threw at each other.

It occurs to me that Oklahoma may have deserved the man it voted into office.

In any case, one of the problems generated by the state's executive office was this: before he was elected, Walton had promised a job in advance to every man who asked for one. When most of these men showed up and asked Walton to make good on his promise, usually there were several persons applying for the same position. For example, two newly appointed presidents, one of whom had never progressed past high school level, claimed the office at the agricultural college in Stillwater. Most of the faculty and student body walked out in protest. This was a typical situation throughout the state.

Each day Daddy recorded the court proceedings, all of which had to be transcribed, printed, and set out on the legislators' desks the next day. The governor — no doubt fearing exposure — imposed a midnight curfew, locked out the legislators, and backed up his decree with armed soldiers. One final night they chased and shot at Daddy, who later on told us they had wanted his notes. The soldiers were poor shots: the records were in place the next day and Walton was successfully impeached. But only after the sheriff deputized many more men to stop the soldiers.

Charles Edward Carter, Daddy, court reporter at Walton's trial.

My Parents:
Charlie and Cosie Carter

My PARENTS, Charles E. Carter (1887–1939) and Cosette Keegan (1882–1973) were devoted sweethearts during all their years together. They even had a special whistle to announce their arrival home to one another.

Daddy, five years younger than Mother, was frail all his life long, and when he died so young at the age of fifty-two, how Mother missed him! He had a short and delicate frame, resembling more his mother than his six-foot father. Mother and son even shared the same hobbies: gardening and writing poetry.

Mother (Cosie) spent some of her childhood on a small Kansas farm, keeping up with her mischief-making brothers. She grew to be a feisty woman, and that robust quality of spirit shows in photographs taken throughout her entire life. Grandfather used to say that as an infant she kicked the slats out of her cradle! She had four or five years more of education than Daddy, and upon graduating, taught kindergarten for several years.

Though scarlet fever had obliged Daddy to cut short his education, he was the scholar and the reader. Ever ambitious and always successful, he achieved his high aims in his home town of South Bend, Indiana, as well as elsewhere throughout the course of his varied careers.

Mother was satisfied just to be with her husband. Once, when he was leasing farmland for an oil company south of Oklahoma City, she took out a license as a notary public so that she could spend more time with him.

It was Mother who largely supervised our education

Charles E. Carter, 1887–1939

Cosette Carter, 1882–1973

and she also saw to it that all three of her daughters were musically literate. Cosie herself played the mandolin, and enough piano to be able to accompany her kindergarten students, whom she taught both before and after my parents were married in Shawnee, Oklahoma, in 1908.

The photograph on the cover of this book was taken of Mother and her older brother Ed, to "prove" that the latter was musical. Actually, Ed was tone-deaf, as was his mother, but nonetheless Grandmother Ida would sit beaming with pride as she listened to us, her three granddaughters, play our instruments. She couldn't tell one note from another any better than Ed could.

Mother's tasks were teaching school and raising three young daughters, while Daddy was away much of that time. I was the eldest of the three, born in 1910, with the birth of my sisters, Gene and Alice, following within five years of my own. Gene was a tomboy, Alice the youngest and most innocent, and myself the one most in love with books. But in fact, the pristine beauty of the Oklahoma open air and the magical lure of childhood curiosity kept all of us outdoors hard at play, and Mother was obliged to make all three of us pants outfits to keep us reasonably clean.

Back in the early days of their marriage, Charlie and Cosie were so poor that they rented out one story of their home in order to make payments, and then furnished their own half of the house with boxes. But lack of funds never held them back. Again and again throughout the years, they "traded up": sometimes building a new house while living in an unfinished one in the meantime. One house had no dining room floor during the entire three months that we lived there.

Cosie in her first leg-o-mutton sleeves, playing her mandolin;
Ed was tone-deaf like Grandma, so he learned one tune on the
guitar, then had the picture made just to prove he could play it.

The last few years of their life together, the family lived in a dream house called "The Gainsborough." It was located in an exclusive district of Oklahoma City, near the new state capitol building. It was the first home in the neighborhood to have air-conditioning: a tub full of ice in the attic, set underneath a fan, with furnace ducts to carry cool air throughout the rest of the house. This was a luxury that in later years was to lure more than one of our beaux during the hot sizzling summers of Oklahoma.

Daddy's delicate health culminated in two years of illness, during four months of which he was hospitalized. He met his troubles with his usual good humor:

"At least we're cashing in on all that health insurance!"

Mother had loved the house, but when Daddy died, she walked away from it without a backward glance. She let it go for tax purposes.

*　*　*　*　*

Charles Carter passed a whole lifetime in fast-paced achievement. During his teens in South Bend, Indiana, he taught himself how to type, invented a short-hand system, which he taught in his own school, and jointly published a book with another teacher entitled *The Crum-Carter Shorthand System*. In Kansas he was secretary to a railroad official until poor health obliged him to move to Oklahoma. Besides having had a bout with scarlet fever, he came from a family with a history of tuberculosis.

Ever health-conscious, my father saw to it that we always slept outdoors on a sleeping porch during both winters and summers, and he took us on long summer trips in an open Dodge touring car. For years we had a

Beautiful Residence Purchased

"The Gainesboro" on East Eighteenth Street

Purchase by Charles E. Carter of "The Gainesborough," a two-story brick residence at 733 East Eighteenth street, Lincoln Terrace, was announced Saturday by G. A. Nichols, Inc. Carter is general superintendent of the Indian Territory Illuminating Oil company for the Oklahoma City district and head of the land department for western Oklahoma. He has been living at 828 East Eighth street. Sale of the house was made by C. J. Scheetz.

The house was constructed late 1928, and, because of its English architecture, was christened "The Gainesborough" for the famous English painter of that name. Consideration of the transaction was not made public.

Daddy with his three girls, posing for the picture. I am to the right, Gene to the left, and Alice on his lap, on the steps of our Beard St. house, Shawnee.

cabin in the Rocky Mountains, at the foot of Pike's Peak, and there we passed many a summertime idyll. The population of the town, Cascade, was about fifty to one hundred fifty people then.

For a number of years Daddy was employed as a court reporter, attending court sessions in Chandler, Oklahoma, just north of Shawnee, where we lived during that period. In those days, before we moved to the capital city, and while Daddy also served as secretary to Lieutenant Governor Trapp, we often used to travel forty miles to Oklahoma City, back and forth.

Cosie kept herself active while Charles was gone: she participated in the Ladies' Aid Society, Eastern Star, and the P.E.O. When Charles was home they enjoyed playing bridge.

Mother taught us not to fear. She introduced us to "Mr. Wind" when he howled down the chimney; she led us out onto the porch during storms, to show us how the trees danced and to see the patterns of lightning in the darkened skies. She spoke ill of no one, and always told us: "If you can't say something good, say nothing at all."

I have always appreciated the childhood that my parents gave me, and not least the example of the way they lived their own lives.

The first stroke of tragic disability struck my father in 1920 or 1921. After years of taking notes in court, a case of writer's cramp became so acute that he finally lost the use of his right hand, and thus the means of his livelihood as well. Undaunted, he sat at our round dining room table, took up our school penmanship manual, and taught himself to write and do shorthand with his left hand. He couldn't achieve sufficient speed to

Main Street, Shawnee, Oklahoma Territory, 1896

continue as a reporter, however.

After so many years of working in law courts and in real estate, it surprised no one when Daddy took up the study of law. Working with great zeal, he passed the bar exams in 1920. He used his credentials as an attorney to help him get an early start in the oil business, a relatively new field then booming in Oklahoma, while the rest of the country was moving into a deep depression. Having already seen so much behind-the-scenes shenanigans among attorneys, Daddy never for one moment actually considered practicing law.

Dealing in oil royalties, he became head land man for ITIO, the Indian Territory Illuminating Oil and Gas Company. From there he went on to become president of one royalty company, and then founder of another. Today the latter is owned by a grand-nephew in Oklahoma City.

On Thanksgiving Day, 1928, our family stood together on the floor of the Discovery Well of the new Oklahoma City oil field, as geologists tested the core and announced that the ITIO had a well. Daddy broadcast that news at a football game that same afternoon, from high in the press box in the bleachers. It was the first well in what proved to be the greatest high gravity oil field in the mid-continent area. Two of the wells in the field eventually produced forty-three thousand barrels of oil a day, thus establishing it as the largest high gravity oil field in the world.

In 1928 Charles was chosen as the "Most Useful Citizen" in Oklahoma City, in recognition of his successful work in checker-boarding the leases in the field, work which had brought so much wealth to the city. Not one lawsuit had been filed by farmers whose land had been leased, a remarkable testimony to his sense of fair play, since the forty-acre consolidated units he assembled left only every other farmer with a producing well on his land.

Our family was rich for two years until an oil glut (overproduction) forced Governor "Alfalfa Bill" Murray to shut down the field. Oil prices dropped to a penny a barrel. Having lots of money was fun while it lasted — not long enough to cause us to become spoiled by the wealth, but as John D. Rockefeller once said: "I've been rich and I've been poor, but rich is better." What was best about it for us was the good education it afforded us, and the fact that it led me to meet my husband-to-be on a trip abroad.

* * * * *

An amusing story that my family has enjoyed retelling is about a telegram that Daddy once sent us in 1930 about a gusher, when he was back in Oklahoma City and the rest of the family was staying at our mountain cabin in Colorado. The wire was hand-carried up a mountain road to us, relayed from the hotel telephone, which was the only one in town.

"Mary Sudik running wild. Two hundred million gasser," is what the telegram said, provoking considerable curiosity among townfolk in Cascade.

"Who is Mary Sudik, and why is she wild?" everyone was wondering.

In the 1920s and 1930s in Oklahoma, oil wells were named for the families on whose farms they were drilled. Three years before, the Sudiks, a Bohemian family, had been stubborn about signing a lease that would give the oil company rights for drilling on their land. It was Uncle

This caption ran in the Daily Oklahoman *newspaper in 1928. The Mary Sudik well ran wild in the Oklahoma City oilfield in 1930. Courtesy of Archives & Manuscripts Division of Oklahoma Historical Society.*

Homer Keegan, Mother's younger brother, who had been the lease man obliged to spend weeks wooing the Sudiks for their consent. Mother happened to be along with him, serving as notary, on the evening when the Sudiks finally gave in and signed. They had been savvy traders. They'd had my uncle to dinner and given him a sack of pecans from the farm, but still they'd held off signing through ten or eleven calls, biding their time.

Finally Homer's boss delivered an ultimatum:

"Go out there today and get that lease, or don't come back." That evening, the Sudiks again had Homer to supper, and late that night close to midnight, after the Sudiks had finished their chores, the four of them drove out to the county line, and with Mother acting as notary, Homer finally won the stubborn farmers over. The headlights of the car provided the light by which the Sudiks signed the lease.

Little did Mary Sudik dream that this would result in her name streaming in headlines all over the world. Over two years later, on March 26, 1930, the well came in and was out of control, creating a stir that no one would ever forget. It ran wild for eleven days before the well was capped. Gas and oil spurted high in the sky, and oil spewed as far as Norman, fifteen miles away. Its fame spread all over the States and abroad, and photographers and newsmen came from afar to cover the event.

Daddy knew that we'd want to know the moment the well blew in, and just how big a gusher it was. The Mary Sudik was part of our family history.

The whole family gathered for Grandmother Mary Carter's funeral. They are, left to right, Eli Carter, Zenas, Will, Cora, Abby, Charles, Milton, Roy, and Ray; South Bend, Indiana.

LIVE TODAY

We live today, why worry 'bout tomorrow,
The sun is shining, 'though the clouds obscure
Today is ours, bringing its joy or sorrow,
Throw out your chest — learn to live today.

Why grieve about mistakes left far behind us.
Our countless troubles in such vast array;
The birds are singing, let our hearts be laughing,
Stick out your chin — learn to live today.

Don't worry 'bout the problems just before you.
They soon will be victories of yesterday;
Just do your best and solve them when arriving,
Display a smiling face — learn to live today.

Count up the ones who've gone before you,
Count up your many blessings, day by day;
The world is yours to conquer, so be fearless,
Time passes on, so — learn to live today.

                                        Charles Edward Carter

Three Sisters

HALLEY'S CHILD
Halley's child I was, born at its zenith
Half between the mother earth and sun,
Comet filling darkened sky with glory,
Thrilling all who watched, its story
Told on every tongue.
Yet one
Bit of human flesh stayed on when the last small
Tag of scintillating light had disappeared
Into the spangled dark of night.

In '86 its glow will shine again,
And where will Halley's child be then? Filling
The same small spot on earth, barely,
Or joining in its cosmic race once more
Between material and celestial shores?

Who knows where beauty leads? I follow,
Whether it be pedestrian or soaring
Speed through endless space, tomorrow's way
To yesterday, in unknown flight.

Virginia Stumbough

T oday we three sisters — Alice, Gene, and Virginia —
are linked on a solid foundation bequeathed to us by loving parents. At age seventy-eight, eighty-one, and
eighty-three, we live far apart, in New York, Texas, and
Idaho, but are in close touch by phone, mail, and in spirit.

One of us is an Episcopalian. A psychic healer, she has

Virginia Carter

Alice Carter

Left to Right: Gene, Alice, and Virginia

Gene Carter

privately published several editions of a booklet entitled, *Pray Without Ceasing* (1975). These are messages she has received from Francis of Assisi, through meditation. In two lines of one of the meditations he says: "Place your trust in the Lord; One Will only. . . . Pray without ceasing for your protection. Let the light lead you always with peace and assurance."

Another one of us is a Unitarian and a student of Edgar Cayce, the psychic healer. The third is a Southern Baptist and respects the other two enough not to pressure them to follow her way to salvation.

But our youthful memories are the same — poverty or plenty scarcely affecting us one way or the other. We remember eating second-day bread, and wearing the hand-me-down clothes of more affluent relatives. We also remember a beautiful house, servants, several cars, and first-class accommodations on a two-month family tour of Europe. We traveled every summer, beginning back in the days when there were no paved roads or road maps. We motored in an open Dodge touring car, and camped at night when there were no campgrounds.

We have our individual ups and downs, like everyone. But nothing can ever divide us, for Mother and Daddy gave us security: fine education, music and books at home, a thorough understanding of how other folk live. Above all they gave us love.

Women in our family are long-lived: one cousin is 102, an aunt is 97, two ancestors lived to 102 and 104. But whether we follow in the family tradition of longevity, or whether we are still breathing or not, we sisters will always be close.

My mother, Cosette, my father, Charles with Gene and myself

My mother and sisters are in our garden, Left to right, with my mother are Alice, Gene, and myself, Virginia.

Flies

TRAVELING IN THE WEST seventy years ago with my family, over hot, dusty roads in an open Dodge touring car, flies weren't much of a problem as long as Mother washed off our sticky fingers and faces after a treat of orange pop.

Cousin Cosette Patrick remembered that as a child, sometimes it was her duty to stand by the dining table at mealtimes and shoo away the flies with a long peacock feather. At times there were two tables, one for adults and one for children. She stood between them, swishing away, left to right, right to left. The dishes of honey, butter, and sweet pickles were all protected with their own covers, but big cut-glass pitchers of lemonade and apple cider were not.

Great Uncle Mart Patterson told us that fly swatters were invented in his lifetime, but during his reign as a householder they apparently had not yet become commonplace. Every year as soon as fly season began, a neighbor borrowed my uncle's swatter and didn't return it until the season's end. Mart was always amused, and without his swatter he continued to swat with a rolled-up newspaper.

Granddaughter Kim and her husband Clay Meeks live on a highly scientific pig farm, out in the countryside in Arkansas. They have installed an ingenious "Electronic Fly Zapper" in the patio, where its light attracts insects to their doom on an electric grill.

In our own home the method of fly control doesn't depend solely on window screens, nor do we resort to the use of a zapper. Years ago, while visiting our home,

Homer Keegan with Gene, Virginia, Mother Cosette, and Alice Carter, in front of our Dodge sedan, on one of our trips West, at Berthod Pass, Colorado, between 1920 and 1922.

Emma Hausnecht, head nurse at the jungle hospital of Dr. Albert Schweitzer at Lambarene in French Equatorial Africa, taught us Dr. Schweitzer's method of catching flies. One approaches the fly directly on the window or curtain so that air movement won't disturb it. Then one claps a paper cup over it, slips a card underneath, and carries the fly outdoors to freedom.

Why not? It works, the fly escapes, and we feel pretty good about it. After all, Dr. Schweitzer was a Nobel Prize winner. Who are we to quarrel with his respect for even the least of us living creatures? His basic philosophy of "reverence for life" extended from mankind to all living beings, including insects.

A Journalist Remembers:
Will Rogers and Dr. Albert Schweitzer

MY EXPERIENCES AS A journalist remain vivid with
memories of the many remarkable personalities that I
have encountered throughout my seventy-year career. I remember an interview with Roald Amundsen, the explorer
who first reached the South Pole, and there was also an
unforgettable meeting with John McCormack, the operatic
tenor, so delightfully full of Irish blarney. I was a high
school student when I talked to him for the *Daily Oklahoman.* The rewrite man hashed my gushy story — I
adored the tenor, and said so — and he put a critical
headline on it. I was heartbroken and wrote Mr. McCormack a tearful letter, saying that I was going to quit
journalism if things like that could happen. And that gra-
cious man answered:

"You must learn to take the bitter with the sweet, and
that life is not all a bed of roses." It takes a great man to
take the time to comfort a fifteen-year-old girl.

Too, there was a missed chance with Charles Lind-
bergh because I was too overawed and shy to approach
the famous aviator.

But there were two people whom I never met in actual-
ity, much less interviewed, whose presence and example
have long moved me in a profound and lasting way. These
were Will Rogers, the beloved Oklahoman columnist and
humorist, and Dr. Albert Schweitzer, the jungle doctor
and recipient of the Nobel Peace Prize.

On April 22, 1929, forty thousand people gathered in
Ponca City, Oklahoma to honor the dauntless spirit of our

early homesteaders. The unveiling ceremony of the Pioneer Woman statue was to signal the culmination of the event, and though there were plenty of dignitaries on hand for the occasion, the presence of Will Rogers was the main attraction. Like those who gathered around Mahatma Gandhi in India, drawn to him by his aura of goodness, tens of thousands of Oklahomans came to share and bask in the warmth of the dearly esteemed personality of their favorite native son.

We were a quiet expectant crowd, waiting patiently in the hot sun for Will's turn to speak. Few of us had ever seen him in person, but we faithfully read his daily newspaper column, heard him speak on the radio, and we all saw his films. We'd heard that in order for Will to be with us, back in Hollywood he had paid the extras seven thousand dollars a day out of his own pocket, as reimbursement for the time lost in shooting his current film. We weren't surprised: he was family, our dear friend: of course he would be there.

First there were speeches broadcast over the radio, from both President Herbert Hoover and Secretary of War, Pat Hurley, another Oklahoma native. Next, we waited through the speeches of Governor William Hollaway; sculptor Bryant Baker, who had created the statue; and the oil magnate who had funded it, E. W. Marland. We could not begrudge these worthy men their participation, but there was no question as to who the real star of the event was going to be.

Finally, Will appeared, chewing gum and grinning at us all, as we strained forward to hear. He did not wear a top hat like the others. His opening remarks were:

"Now that the applesauce and baloney is over, we'll

"THE PIONEER WOMAN" — The monument to "The Pioneer Woman," by Bryant Baker, well known sculptor, was unveiled on the Cherokee Strip, Oklahoma, The monument is thirty-five feet high. I saw the unveiling of this statue. Will Rogers was the speaker. Photo courtesy of Archives and Manuscripts Division of the Oklahoma Historical Society.

PIONEERS
By Lalia Mitchell Thornton

Pioneer women and pioneer men,
There is the need of your courage again.
Life has been easy and days have been clear;
Peace has been with us for many a year;
Now we have watched as the clouds darken fast —
You threw off the yoke, must we wear it at last?
Let us remember the work you did then,
Pioneer women and pioneer men.

155

state a few facts. You had to be a crook or you wouldn't be here!"*

Rogers was referring to the fact that "Boomer-Sooner" pioneers illegally beat the gun when Oklahoma Territory opened to settlement sixty-two years before, in the historic run for land in 1889. Indeed, to be one of the victors in that race required a fearless determination which didn't hesitate to "squeeze through" certain legalities. Fifty years later Will Rogers, Jr. wrote, "As the Sooner State, Oklahoma is the only state to point to an illegal act as a matter of pride."**

The audience that the original Will Rogers was addressing was largely composed of those feisty pioneers themselves, or at the very least, Oklahomans with plenty of the pioneer genes! Will continued:

"I'm pinch-hitting for the governor, in case he is impeached before the thing is over. Oklahoma takes its census by a man standing outside the capitol and counting the governors as they come out (Governor Walton's impeachment had taken place in Oklahoma only six years earlier. The scandal was still in the air, though sufficiently distant in time for Rogers' remark to be both humorous and fresh. And obviously, approved).

"I sure appreciate Marland's inviting me to this affair, so I can get to see the inside of his home." This remark referred to the open house that was being held at the mansion of the oil magnate that day. Rogers continues,

---

* From the personal journal of Virginia Stumbough.
**Will Rogers, Jr., Foreword to Marcia Keegan's, *Oklahoma,* New York: Abbeville Press, 1979.

Will Rogers. Courtesy of Archives and Manuscripts Division of the Oklahoma Historical Society.

the same irreverent vein, sparing none:

"This crowd looks like an Osage payment [this refers to the days when Indians gathered on reservations to collect their quarterly allotments from the government]. It's the biggest since the Walton barbecue. I'm just here to act the fool for the home folks. If it had been a modern woman I wouldn't have come; no one would, she doesn't need any help. . . . That's the cleanest face I ever saw on an Oklahoma boy." The pose of the statue is intended to evoke the feeling of striding across the prairie. The woman is holding a young son by one hand, clutching a bundle and a Bible in the other. Will praised the corset she wore, and then branched off and related an appropriate anecdote:

"Why, the other day I sat down on a bench by a woman in a corset, and she was so big and the corset so tight, that she just edged me over, and first thing I knew I was pushed off that bench. . . . I have a wonderful wife. She's the only woman in the world, I'm sure, who would let her husband go fifteen hundred miles to take the clothes off another woman."

Six years later Will died as he was embarking on an airborne jaunt, intending to explore the Alaskan coast with the famous and foolhardy one-eyed pilot, Wiley Post. Taking off in fog from a gas stop, with pontoons that were too large, the tiny overweighted plane nose-dived and crashed immediately. Thirty days later, Will's much beloved wife, Mary, passed away, seemingly for no other cause than a profound grieving for the loss of her lifelong mate. Indeed, grief for Will's untimely death was world-wide, for I was not the only one who ran down the street crying, to share my sorrow with the neighbors. We loved you, Will. We miss you.

*　*　*　*　*

Dr. Albert Schweitzer, one of the noblest men of our times, is credited with having spread the concept, "reverence for life." What does it mean?

Speaking in August, 1990, at the United Nations, on the occasion of an Albert Schweitzer Colloquium, Dr. William Foege gave the following interpretation: "The final criterion for measuring civilization is not found in knowledge, science, technology, happiness, legal structures, freedom or even health. The final measure is how people treat each other."*

Norman Cousins said of Schweitzer that he had hoped that people who had themselves been delivered from physical suffering would in turn respond to those similarly in need. Cousins went on to cite the need for each of us to recognize the same noble instinct within ourselves, identify with those who have less, and especially with the most vulnerable among us — our children.

The following is the story of how the pure intentions of a small group of children inspired a further benevolence around them. That is, through the children's example of uncontrived and simple generosity, the instinct to give and rejoice in the giving was awakened in others.

During World War II an article in *Look* magazine made reference to the fact that there was no soap to be had in certain children's hospitals abroad. One eventual result of

---

* *Reverence*, published by the Albert Schweitzer Center, Great Barrington, Mass., November, 1990.

159

that publicity was an annual gift of soap to Dr. Schweitzer, as a gesture to help in implementing his vision. The magnitude of this gift escalated in a few years so that the final shipment to his hospital contained over five thousand bars of soap.

But it didn't start out that way. The first shipment was of two dozen bars, and it wasn't sent to Africa then, nor to Dr. Schweitzer.

In Evanston, Illinois, back in December of 1948, my children and a half dozen of their friends wanted to go caroling. I agreed to take them around the neighborhood on Christmas Eve, and in the preceding days we practiced diligently so that we would know all the words.

It turned out to be a lot of fun, but I was somewhat upset with their "trick-or-treat" attitude, which compared the goodies passed out at one house with those at another. They were greedy, not giving. I told them that that was the end of caroling. I'd not take them again.

But they didn't give up so easily, so when they asked for caroling the next year, I told them about the children's hospitals with no soap. Would they be willing to forego candy and cookies at the doors, and ask for a bar of soap instead, explaining why we wanted it?

They were enthusiastic, as were the neighbors, and that first year the children chose to send the soap to a hospital in Lichtenstein: I'd told them they would receive a thank you letter for sending the soap, and they liked the fancy postage stamps of this country.

The following year they had heard about Dr. Schweitzer's hospital in Lambarene, French Equatorial Africa, and decided to send the soap there. The neighbors expected us this year and had boxes of soap ready for us,

Dr. Albert Schweitzer. Photo by Erica C. Anderson

piled under the trees. They were delighted to learn that the bars were going to be sent to Dr. Schweitzer.

Later, when a thank you letter arrived from him, written in French, I sat down and cried for joy. That evening I took the letter to choir practice and showed it to the choir members and our minister, Dr. Homer Jack. He was enthusiastic, and began to think about what he could do for the hospital too. He was inspired to visit Dr. Schweitzer and ended up working in his hospital for a while. Eventually Dr. Jack wrote about the doctor's good works.

Year after year we continued to send soap to Dr. Schweitzer's hospital. City newspapers and a national magazine publicized our annual "ritual," and when Dr. Schweitzer's head nurse, Miss Emma Hausnecht, visited us in the course of a trip to America to buy hospital supplies, she brought us autographed pictures from the doctor and spoke at our church. Those who attended were of all denominations and of none — we were brought together in our rejoicing in the practice of generosity — the common ground from which all goodness generates and expands.

One year during World War II, we waded through deep snow to carol for soldiers who were stationed on the shore of Lake Michigan, manning anti-aircraft guns. Of this occasion Dr. Schweitzer said how especially happy he was to think of our gathering together in the snow, our songs of praise and appreciation of the Christ child inspiring a further offering of soap for the children in Africa. To each child in the leper colony he distributed a half bar of soap and a bowl of rice, the first Christmas presents they had ever received.

When I read of what a burden Dr. Schweitzer's correspondence had become and subsequently asked him not to write us anymore, he instead added brief notes in French to the long letters his nurses continued to write in English. I added these notes to a big scrapbook of newspaper and magazine articles about the doctor and his hospital, and have since passed it on to one of the Schweitzer libraries. Included in the scrapbook is the text of a filmstrip that I published about Dr. Schweitzer and his work.

When my family moved to the mountains in Colorado in 1956, we tried caroling the first year, but the mountain slopes were too steep, the snow too deep, and the houses too far apart. When I mentioned to a former fellow Oklahoman, George Knox, how sorry I was that we could no longer continue to send soap, his response was on the dot: "But Virginia," said George, "don't you know that I have a mail order business for personalized soap? I'll be happy to donate returned orders and discontinued styles to Dr. Schweitzer's cause."

The good man did indeed do so, and in such profusion that shipping and costs became a problem. That obstacle was solved by community appeals and cooperative effort: Boy Scouts made boxes; members of the Council of Churches transported them down to Colorado Springs; factories banded the boxes with the metal bands required by law; a freight company then sent them to New York free of charge; and finally, a Schweitzer foundation sent them overseas.

The last shipment, sent just before Mr. Knox's soap business shut down, contained five thousand bars of soap. On the wall by our piano is an autographed photograph of Dr. Schweitzer and one of his last letters, written in French.

When our minister, Dr. Jack from Evanston, was stepping into a canoe on the Ogowe River and bidding good-bye to Lamborene, Dr. Schweitzer had this to say: "I have another friend in Evanston. Do you know Mrs. Stumbough?" and thereupon gave Dr. Jack a fork and spoon set, hand-carved in ebony by the natives, to pass on to me. I never met the doctor, musician, philosopher, clergyman, missionary, author, Nobel Peace Prize winner . . . but we were friends.

Today's Pioneers

THE WOMEN IN OUR families have always been pioneers. Like thousands of other European immigrants fleeing harsh times in the old country, Catherine Flanigan Keegan (1778–1874), Patrick Henry's mother, sailed from Ireland to a foreign land whose customs were sometimes utterly strange to her. Sarah Ann Mulholland's mother, Abigail Choate, left a life of affluence in Belfast for the wilderness of Indiana.

These women were "just housewives." But read of Abigail Jane Keegan's daily tasks in a homestead near Macy, Indiana, and the concept of housewife broadens, and prefacing it with "just" becomes unthinkable.

My grandmother Ida Keegan ran the first United Provident Association in Shawnee, Oklahoma. My mother Cosette Keegan taught the first kindergarten in Oklahoma Territory. In 1933, another woman and myself were the first to graduate from the University of Oklahoma with master's degrees in journalism — only to be told subsequently by male editors: "We don't hire women."

In 1961, my daughter was one of the first thirteen women in the United States to pass the advanced astronaut tests, and then — perhaps a legacy of hardship from the past — she was told that the woman's program had been killed. What follows is Nora Gene's own pioneer story, a fairly unique and impressive one by anyone's standards, not just her mother's!

The Stumbough family, White Hall, Illinois. Gertrude, Winona, Ella, Harold, John Riley, Elmer and baby Bill my husband's parents, sisters, and brothers, about 1910–1911. I married Harold in 1933.

Gene Nora Jessen, Pilot

"Oh, Mother," Gene Nora protested, in anticipating the way I would be describing some of the facts of her life. "Everyone thinks that every race you fly in is a 'Powder Puff Derby', and if you fly long enough, the story grows until it's told you won them all! I've been flying for forty years — how are you going to manage to stick to the facts?"

Well, it's not easy. For one thing, how do you describe your only daughter without sounding smarmy? She is a tall woman, and dresses in skirts and heels, even when flying. Especially when flying. Personally, I wear pants to keep my legs warm, and my idea of style is to match the colors of my hat and necklace. I believe my daughter learned to dress beautifully when she was in public relations, working seven years for Beech Aircraft as their sales representative and demonstration pilot. She flew their Musketeer plane all over the country when it was just being marketed, and no doubt her elegant appearance effortlessly demonstrated to skeptical males how easy it is for women to fly.

Today she owns her own Beech Bonanza, and before that had a rebuilt Musketeer, a little red plane with her name on it. Her two young nephews called it "Aunt Gene Nora's Mustard Ear."

As Admiral John Hawkins broke barriers in the sea, Gene Nora has broken barriers in her own sky-bound milieu. Though the only girl in the corps, she had been a pilot since she was a Cadet Commandant of the Civil Air Patrol in Evanston Township High School in Illinois. By college she knew where she was headed, and chose the

University of Oklahoma because of its school of aviation. By her third year she had earned a place as flight instructor.

As a woman in an often all-male field, she proved that with determination and innate ability, her goal of becoming a pilot was feasible. She "flew" to the top. Viewing it from the sidelines, it looked like hard, unending work all the way. However, I do believe that Gene Nora enjoyed the process and felt that the goal was worth the sometimes painful barriers that she broke.

Flight school was costly. She worked as a student during her undergraduate years, took summer jobs, and sometimes dropped out of school for a while to work. It took six and a half years to earn her degree, along with the flight training. By that time she had logged fifteen hundred hours in the air, thus qualifying as a commercial pilot and certified flight instructor.

She also joined The Ninety-Nines, Inc., a worldwide organization of fifteen thousand licensed women pilots, for whom she served as international president from 1988 until 1990.

Gene Nora qualified to participate in an arduous six-day physical test for women astronauts, which won her the right to be one of thirteen women to go on for advanced tests. As already mentioned, the program, which by the way had cost the government ten thousand dollars each, was dropped. The excellent results of their tests was kept secret until 1962, when *Life* magazine told the story:

"The United States could have been the first [country] to put a woman in space merely by deciding to do so . . . . All were experienced pilots with qualifications far more impressive than Valentina Tereshkova's (the Russian

Gene Nora Jessen, pilot

cosmonaut). She was not even a pilot and had virtually no technical background."

Gene Nora, aged twenty-six, was the second youngest in the group. NASA was definitely not interested until many years later, in training women to go into space. And when women finally did achieve astronaut status, Nora Gene learned that one of the first women in the program was being instructed by one of her own former pupils.

Of my daughter's many credentials in the field of aviation, there are perhaps two others that must not go unmentioned: she was appointed by President Johnson to the Federal Aviation Administration's Women's Advisory Committee on Aviation, and she served for ten years on the Boise Airport Commission.

Needless to say, she has passed on the craft and love of flying to her own daughter. We can rejoice that there are now tens of thousands of women pilots, and that the obstacles to pursuing their paths have been somewhat diminished through the confident persistence of women aviators and pioneers such as my daughter, Gene Nora Jessen.

Afterword

THIS IS A BOOK of American history in the making as it was lived by real people, moving toward the forms and conventions of today, informed by those of the past. Your own family stories are just as clearly the raw material of lived history. You have the ability to prevent this history from slipping away, the opportunity to preserve a unique and perishable legacy.

One book such as this cannot tell it all, but it can serve to remind each of us that there is more — untapped sources of stories, events, traditions, characters, and places.

As I think of the stories I've told here, other memories and associations well up. I remember my 102-year-old cousin's description of the covered bridge in her town where, if you were agile enough, you could climb to the rafters and find her father's initials carved there. The three sisters who remember a week-long, cross-country train ride during World War I . . . how their mother dressed them in black to camouflage the soot that covered their clothes as it came through the open windows . . . the daily stops for meals at Harvey Houses. And how about the letters of an aunt describing her own long ride to one of the first Rose Parades in Portland, Oregon, when fellow passengers entertained one another with singing and stunts.

Do you remember the patent medicine ads on the backs of cardboard fans distributed to every customer under the blistering hot canvas tent when the Chautauqua* came to town, bringing "culture" to the back country? Or perhaps you once watched a young person go up to the famous evangelist Aimé Semple McPherson's altar on crutches, returning to the pew without them after her laying-on of hands. And what do you remember about the street vendors passing by your house? Was there a hot tamale man or an ice-cream wagon? Did the ice man let you suck on the shards of dripping ice? What about the collector of old rags and bones — do you remember him?

Your older relatives are a precious living legacy. Many of them may be delighted to go through drawers, trunks and attics with you. Take down their stories about mementos saved through the generations. More important, take down the stories of what they remember themselves: both the odd and fanciful random memories, as well as the vivid and bold, unforgettable ones. Collect the letters they have bothered to save all these years.

You are the keeper of your family's history; no one else can tell it in such detail. Never mind if you feel unable to write these stories well. Use your tape recorder and take notes. Save your family stories before it's too late, for they are a lode of riches we can't afford to lose. Don't forget to put names and dates on the backs of photographs. Identify the people: are they related or only good friends? Your grandchildren won't know. "Compost" these memories, for they may one day fertilize a rich crop. At the very least, you can donate them to an historical museum or society.

Good luck to you in the digging.

---

* A traveling lecture and entertainment show.

Now I am a great-grandmother and am eighty-three years old with many good family memories.